TRAVERSE
THEATRE

Traverse Theatre Company

Abandonment
by Kate Atkinson

cast in order of appearance

Agnes	Michelle Gomez
Elizabeth	Patricia Kerrigan
Suzy/Gertie	Kathryn Howden
Kitty/Laetitia	Elaine C Smith
Callum/Rev Scobie	James Cunningham
Ina/Lavender	Sheila Reid
Alec/Merric	Neil McKinven

director	John Tiffany
designer	Georgia Sion
lighting designer	Ben Ormerod
composer	John Irvine
stage manager	Gavin Harding
deputy stage ma	
assistant stage ma	
wardrobe supe	
wardrobe ass	

D1419860

dresser	Stephanie Thorburn

First performed at the Traverse Theatre
Tuesday 11 July 2000

TRAVERSE THEATRE

One of the most important theatres in Britain The Observer

Edinburgh's **Traverse Theatre** is Scotland's new writing theatre, with a 37 year record of excellence. With quality, award-winning productions and programming, the Traverse receives accolades at home and abroad from audiences and critics alike.

The Traverse has an unrivalled reputation for producing contemporary theatre of the highest quality, invention and energy, commissioning and supporting writers from Scotland and around the world and facilitating numerous script development workshops, rehearsed readings and public writing workshops. The Traverse aims to produce several major new theatre productions plus a Scottish touring production each year. It is unique in Scotland in its exclusive dedication to new writing, providing the infrastructure, professional support and expertise to ensure the development of a sustainable and relevant theatre culture for Scotland and the UK.

Traverse Theatre Company productions have been seen worldwide including London, Toronto, Budapest and New York. Recent touring successes in Scotland include PERFECT DAYS by Liz Lochhead, PASSING PLACES by Stephen Greenhorn, HIGHLAND SHORTS, HERITAGE by Nicola McCartney and LAZYBED by Iain Crichton Smith. PERFECT DAYS also played the Vaudeville Theatre in London's West End in 1999. In 2000 the Traverse co-produced Michel Tremblay's SOLEMN MASS FOR A FULL MOON IN SUMMER with London's Barbican Centre, with performances in both Edinburgh and London.

The Traverse can be relied upon to produce more good-quality new plays than any other Fringe venue
Daily Telegraph

During the Edinburgh Festival the Traverse is one of the most important venues with world class premieres playing daily in the two theatre spaces. The Traverse regularly wins awards at the Edinburgh Festival Fringe, including recent *Scotsman Fringe Firsts* for Traverse productions KILL THE OLD TORTURE THEIR YOUNG by David Harrower and PERFECT DAYS by Liz Lochhead.

An essential element of the Traverse Company's activities takes place within the educational sector, concentrating on the process of playwriting for young people. The Traverse flagship education project CLASS ACT offers young people in schools the opportunity to work with theatre professionals and see their work performed on the Traverse stage. In addition the Traverse Young Writers group, led by professional playwrights, has been running for over three years and meets weekly.

Kate Atkinson

KATE ATKINSON was born in Yorkshire and studied English Literature at Dundee University. After graduating in 1974, she worked on a postgraduate doctorate on the American Post-Modern Story in its Historical Context. Kate now lives in Edinburgh.

In 1993 she won the Ian St. James short story competition for *Karmic Mothers - Fact or Fiction?* and shortly after her first novel BEHIND THE SCENES AT THE MUSEUM was published by Transworld. This book went on to win the 1995 Whitbread Book of the Year and became an international bestseller. Her second book HUMAN CROQUET was published in 1997 to wide critical acclaim and also became a number one bestseller. Her third book EMOTIONALLY WEIRD, was published in March.

Her short play NICE was produced at the Traverse in 1996 directed by John Tiffany who also directed her screenplay, KARMIC MOTHERS, for the 1997 BBC Tartan Shorts series. ABANDONMENT is her first full-length play for the stage.

BIOGRAPHIES

James Cunningham (*Callum/RevScobie*): Theatre work includes PENETRATOR (Royal Court) TRAINSPOTTING (Citizens'), both performed at the Traverse; CLEANSED (Royal Court); MARABOU STORK NIGHTMARES (Citizens'). Television includes: A MUG'S GAME; PIE IN THE SKY; ROUGHNECKS 2; CASUALTY; WRITERS AND NATION. Film work includes: WAR REQUIEM; SNATCH'D; BUMPIN' THE ODDS plus various short films and pop videos. Currently working on COME ON DIE YOUNG! (Dogma Films).

Michelle Gomez (*Agnes*): Theatre includes: THE MERCHANT OF VENICE, COMMUNIST MANIFESTO (Volcano); THE MASTER BUILDER (Royal Lyceum); TRAINSPOTTING (West End); CAVALCADE, THE DOUBLE, THE PLEASURE MAN (Citizens'); OF BLESSED MEMORY (Kings Head); SLEEP WITH ME (Royal Nationa Theatre). Television work includes: FIRST AND LAST; THE BILL; TAGGART. Film work includes: THE ACID HOUSE; MY WEST; NEW WORLD DISORDER; MILK; THE WRONG BLONDE; TICKS. Michelle is part of The Farm Film Production Company. For them, she produced TICKS which has just been screened at the Greenwich Film Festival and goes on to the Sundance Film Festival.

Kathryn Howden (*Susie/Gertie*): Trained: RSAMD. For the Traverse: PASSING PLACES, BONDAGERS (Traverse & on tour Canada, London, Budapest), THE HOPE SLIDE, BUCHANAN, POOR SUPERMAN (Traverse/ Hampstead). Other theatre work includes: THE GOVERNMENT INSPECTOR (Almeida); NEVER BEFORE SEEN, FAMILIAR, EARTHQUAKE WEATHER, VIPER'S OPIUM (Starving Artists); THE MARRIAGE OF FIGARO, CAN'T PAY? WON'T PAY!, A FAMILY AFFAIR, THE MERCHANT OF VENICE, THE TAMING OF THE SHREW (Royal Lyceum); ROAD, NAE PROBLEM (7:84 Scotland); DANTON'S DEATH (Communicado); JUST FRANK, SHOOTING DUCKS (Theatre Royal, Stratford East); BEAUTY AND THE BEAST, SWING HAMMER SWING (Citizens'); TARTUFFE, LOSING ALEC (Tron); SEX COMEDIES (Old Red Lion). Television work includes: FORGOTTEN, PEAK PRACTICE, AROUND SCOTLAND, MACRAME MAN, LET YOURSELF GO, TAGGART. Tartan Shorts: THE PEN, KARMIC MOTHERS. Film includes: THE PRIEST AND THE PIRATE (V.I.P.). Kathryn is also an experienced radio broadcaster having recorded many plays for BBC Radio Scotland, Radio 3 and Radio Clyde. Writing work has included a commission from the Traverse for SHARP SHORTS.

John Irvine (composer): ABANDONMENT is John's 17th show for the Traverse. Other theatre work includes KtC, Tron Theatre, Dundee Rep, Royal Lyceum, Citizens', TAG, Gate Theatre and Lung Ha's. John works as a composer and teacher in Edinburgh and is currently co-editing an edition of *Contemporary Music Review* on Edgard Varèse with Stephen Davismoon. In the spring of 2001 he will compose the music for the KtC/ Royal Lyceum production of WOYZECK directed by Guy Hollands.

Patricia Kerrigan (*Elizabeth*): Trained: Drama Centre, London. Theatre includes: SHANGALANG (Tour); THE STORM (Almeida); MACBETH (Bristol Old Vic); BEAUTIFUL THING (Bush); TWELFTH NIGHT, LE CID (Cheek by Jowl); ALL'S WELL THAT ENDS WELL, DUCHESS OF MALFI (RSC); LOVES LABOURS LOST, WOMEN LAUGHING (Manchester Royal Exchange); CARTHAGINIANS (Hampstead); DAMON AND PYTHIAS (Shakespeare's Globe). Television work includes: WHERE THE HEART IS; DALZIEL AND PASCOE; BRIGHT HAIR; THE CROW ROAD; FLOWERS OF THE FOREST; A FATAL INVERSION; MEDICS; CASUALTY; PLAYING FOR REAL; TAGGART; SHERLOCK HOLMES; BOON; SHRINKS, THE BILL. Film work includes: THE MAGIC TOYSHOP; JOYRIDERS; AGE OF TREASON; Little Avril in BIG PANTS. Directing includes: THIS DREAM (Actors Centre, London).

Neil McKinven (*Alec/Merric*): Trained: RADA. For the Traverse: WIDOWS. Other theatre work includes: DISSENT, CALEDONIA DREAMING, ROAD (7:84); DEAD FUNNY (Royal Lyceum); WHEN I WAS A GIRL I USED TO SCREAM AND SHOUT (National Tour); THE MARK (Cockpit); RIDDANCE, THE COSMONAUT'S LAST MESSAGE TO THE WOMAN HE ONCE LOVED IN THE FORMER SOVIET UNION (Paines Plough); THE SHIP (Glasgow Docks); OEDIPUS (Theatre Babel). Television includes: TAGGART, STRATHBLAIR, THE SHIP, THE VET, TAKIN' OVER THE ASYLUM, GLASGOW KISS, DEGREES OF ERROR, THE VET. Short films include: COMMISION, WHAT IF?.

Sheila Reid (*Ina/Lavender*): Theatre in Scotland includes: Pinter Season (Traverse); OH WHAT A LOVELY WAR (Royal Lyceum) and a season at Perth Rep. London theatre work includes: OTHELLO, THREE SISTERS, THE BEAUX' STRATAGEM, THE CRUCIBLE, HEDDA GABLER (Royal National Theatre); KING LEAR, THE WOOD DEMON and TARTUFFE (The Actors Company); ROMEO AND JULIET, 'TIS PITY SHE'S A WHORE, KING BABY (RSC); THE GENTLE AVALANCHE, SMALL CHANGE, MY MOTHER SAID I NEVER SHOULD (Royal Court); WHEN I WAS A GIRL I USED TO SCREAM AND SHOUT (Bush, Edinburgh and Whitehall); THE MARSHALLING YARD (Olivier Nomination), ONE FLEA SPARE (Bush); THE WINTER GUEST (West Yorkshire Playhouse and Almeida); THE IMPORTANCE OF BEING EARNEST (Chichester and

Haymarket). Recent musicals include: MARTIN GUERRE (Prince Edward); SWEENEY TODD (RNT); INTO THE WOODS (Donmar Warehouse). Film work includes: THE WINTER GUEST, AMERICAN FRIENDS, SIRE HENRY AT RAWLINSON'S END, BRAZIL, FIVE DAYS ONE SUMMER, FELICIA'S JOURNEY. One woman shows: LOVE AMONG THE BUTTERFLIES, AS DOROTHY PARKER ONCE SAID... (Edinburgh and London). Television work includes leading parts in: TAGGART, DR FINLAY, WHERE THE HEART IS, THE BILL, THE EMMIGRANTS and many more. Recent radio: THE HOUSE, COALVILLE AND SOAMES, VILLETTE and BRISTOW.

Georgia Sion (designer): For the Traverse: PERFECT DAYS (also Hampstead, Vaudeville and tour). Other theatre work includes: TWO CLOUDS OVER EDEN (Royal Exchange); ARABIAN NIGHTS (Young Vic and tour); THE IMPORTANCE OF BEING EARNEST (Nottingham Playhouse); THE COSMONAUT'S LAST MESSAGE TO THE WOMAN HE ONCE LOVED IN THE FORMER SOVIET UNION, CRAVE, SLEEPING AROUND (Paines Plough); CARAVAN (National Theatre of Norway); AFORE NIGHT COME (Theatr Clwyd); THE WEAVERS (Gate); TWELFTH NIGHT (Central School of Speech and Drama); OTHELLO (Watermill/ Tokyo Globe); THE SUNSET SHIP (Young Vic); SHIFT (Old Red Lion); CUT AND RUNNING (Battersea Arts Centre); LOVERS (RSC Fringe Festival); Opera includes: A-RONNE, A MEDICINE FOR MELANCHOLY (ENO Baylis Program); KING AND MARSHAL (Bloomsbury); FOUR SAINTS IN THREE ACTS (Trinity Opera).

Elaine C Smith (*Kitty/Laetitia*): Trained: RSAMD, Glasgow University, Moray House College of Education. Taught at Firrhill High, Edinburgh for 3 years. Joined 7:84 Theatre Company in 1982 and appeared extensively for 15 years with Wildcat, Borderline, Bristol Express, The Byre and Tron Theatre. Original cast of THE STEAMIE and THE GUID SISTERS and has played The Dame for many years at the King's Theatre, Glasgow. She also played Beatrice in MUCH ADO ABOUT NOTHING at the Royal Lyceum. TV and radio work includes: NAKED RADIO, THE USUAL SUSPECTS, many presenting jobs, NAKED VIDEO, CITY LIGHTS, THE LAST WITCH, HUBBUB and 8 series of RAB C NESBITT. Recently completed her first film, WOMEN TALKING DIRTY, with Gina McKee and Helena Bonham Carter. Elaine and her husband run a theatre and TV production company, touring extensively with SHIRLEY VALENTINE and ELAINE WITH ATTITUDE. They are about to start filming a second series of ELAINE for BBC Scotland. Last year the University of Dundee awarded her a Doctorate and she is extremely active in many political and charitable causes. This is her first appearance for the Traverse and during the Fringe Elaine is also appearing in her stand up show HORMONALLY DRIVEN at the Gilded Balloon.

John Tiffany (director): Trained: Glasgow University. Literary Director at the Traverse since June 1997. He directed KING OF THE FIELDS, THE JUJU GIRL, DANNY 306 + ME (4 EVER) (also Birmingham Rep), PERFECT DAYS (also Hampstead, Vaudeville and tour), GRETA, PASSING PLACES (also Citizens' and tour), SHARP SHORTS and co-directed STONES AND ASHES for the Traverse. Other theatre work includes: HIDE AND SEEK and BABY, EAT UP (LookOut); THE SUNSET SHIP (Young Vic); GRIMM TALES (Leicester Haymarket); EARTHQUAKE WEATHER (Starving Artists). Film includes: KARMIC MOTHERS (BBC Tartan Shorts) and GOLDEN WEDDING (BBC Two Lives).

Ben Ormerod (lighting designer): For the Traverse: MAN TO MAN, SHARP SHORTS, PASSING PLACES. Ben began his career with Andrew Visnevski's Cherub company, touring Europe with productions such as Kafka's THE TRIAL before lighting for Deborah Warner's Kick Theatre. As well as designing theatre, opera and dance for the national companies, reps and touring companies throughout the UK, Ben has worked extensively abroad including Greece, Slovenia, Japan, and most recently Ireland where he lit THE BEAUTY QUEEN OF LEENANE for Druid Theatre which he has since taken to London, Broadway, Sydney and Toronto. Forthcoming work includes REMEMBRANCE OF THINGS PAST (Royal National Theatre), HENRY V (RSC), THE BENCH (Theatro Synchrono, Athens) and a new dance piece by Didi Veldman (Gulbenkian Theatre, Lisbon). Ben is also currently lighting The Calico Textiles Museum, Ahmedebad.

For generous help on
Abandonment
the Traverse thanks:

Point Hotel• The Chair Woman Interiors • Camerabase
National Museums of Scotland - Geology Dept.
Imperial Tobacco Ltd • Moet & Chandon Champagne
The Royal Lyceum Theatre • Pitlochry Festival Theatre
Dundee Repertory Theatre • Murray's Tool Stores
The List • Grange Clocks
Allan K. L. Jackson Antiques & Curios • Liz Smith
Mr & Mrs Mellor • Caroline McRae • Mrs Harding
Alaistair Turnbull • Stephen McIlroy
The Edinburgh Cake Shop • BLF • Euan Myles
The Meadows Lamp Gallery • Optical California

LEVER BROTHERS for wardrobe care

Sets, props and costumes for
Abandonment
created by Traverse Workshops
(funded by the National Lottery)

scenic artist Monique Jones
painters Julie Kirsop, Jenny Lau, Siobhan O'Neill
carpentry workshop placement Maja Flygare
placement Alasdair McKay

production photography Kevin Low
print photography Euan Myles

SPONSORSHIP

Sponsorship income enables the Traverse to commission and produce new plays and offer audiences a diverse and exciting programme of events throughout the year.

We would like to thank the following companies for their support throughout the year:

BANK OF SCOTLAND

BBC Scotland

artism

CORPORATE ASSOCIATE SCHEME

LEVEL ONE
Balfour Beatty
Scottish Life the PENSION company
United Distillers & Vintners

LEVEL TWO
Laurence Smith -
Wine Merchants
NB Information
Willis Corroon Scotland Ltd
Wired Nomad

LEVEL THREE
Alistir Tait FGA -
Antiques & Fine Jewellery
Nicholas Groves Raines -
Architects
McCabe Partnership -
Chartered Accountants
KPMG
Scottish Post Office Board

With thanks to

Navy Blue Design, print designers for the Traverse and George Stewarts the printers.

Purchase of the Traverse Box Office, computer network and technical and training equipment has been made possible with money from The Scottish Arts Council National Lottery Fund.

THE SCOTTISH ARTS COUNCIL
National Lottery Fund

The Traverse Theatre's work would not be possible without the support of

THE SCOTTISH ARTS COUNCIL · EDINBVRGH ·
THE CITY OF EDINBURGH COUNCIL

The Traverse receives financial assistance for its educational and development work from

John Lewis Partnership, Peggy Ramsay Foundation, Binks Trust, The Yapp Charitable Trusts, The Bulldog Prinsep Theatrical Trust, Calouste Gulbenkian Foundation, Gannochy Trust, Gordon Fraser Charitable Trust, The Garfield Weston Foundation, The Paul Hamlyn Foundation, JSP Pollitzer Charitable Trust.
The Education Institute of Scotland, supporting arts projects produced by and for children. **EIS**

Charity No. SC002368

ABANDONMENT

Kate Atkinson

A Nick Hern Book

Abandonment first published in Great Britain in 2000
as an original paperback by Nick Hern Books Limited,
14 Larden Road, London W3 7ST, in association with
the Traverse Theatre, Edinburgh

Typeset by Country Setting, Kingsdown, Kent CT14 8ES
Printed and bound in Great Britain by Athenaeum Press Ltd,
Gateshead, Tyne and Wear

A CIP catalogue record for this book is available from the
British Library

ISBN 185459601 2

For John Tiffany

I would like to thank the Traverse Theatre for all the help and support that they gave me during the writing of this play. Gratitude is also due to the actors who contributed to workshops and rehearsals.

Characters

ELIZABETH McMichael
KITTY, *her sister*
INA, *their mother*
SUSIE, *Elizabeth's best friend*
CALLUM INNES, *a builder*
AGNES SOUTAR, *a governess*
ALEC FRAZER, *photographer*
MERRIC CHALMERS, *a lawyer*
LAETITIA, *his wife*
LAVENDER, *his mother*
GERTIE, *their maid*
REVEREND CHARLES SCOBIE

This text went to press before the opening night, and may therefore differ slightly from the play as performed.

ACT ONE

Scene 1

The living-room of a flat in a converted Victorian mansion.
A large window. No carpet on the floor throughout. The place
is in some disarray, packing-cases etc. A piano with old
photographs on top of it and a candle. AGNES sits at the
piano, playing 'Home Sweet Home'. She stops abruptly, blows
out the candle, and leaves.

ELIZABETH (*offstage*). No, I have everything I need, it's okay.

> ELIZABETH *enters, carrying a cardboard box and*
> *switches on the light.* SUSIE, *also carrying a box, enters,*
> *followed by* KITTY, *carrying a bottle of champagne.*

KITTY. God it's wild out there.

SUSIE. I hope it's not bad luck to flit in a storm.

ELIZABETH. Stormy weather.

SUSIE. Mother Nature's in a stushie about something. You
kept the curtains.

ELIZABETH. It would cost a fortune to put up new ones. It's
such a big window.

SUSIE. I do like big windows. It's like . . . I don't know, the
outside world coming in.

ELIZABETH. Not the inside world getting out?

KITTY. You're going to have to get double glazing. And
central heating. And God knows what else. The place is a
wreck. Has it had anything done to it in the past hundred
years?

ELIZABETH. Not much. That's why I liked it.

KITTY. It smells like someone died in here. They're a strange
colour, aren't they? The curtains. What do you call that?

SUSIE. Yellow?

ELIZABETH. I think it's chartreuse.

KITTY. Chartreuse?

ELIZABETH. Chartreuse.

SUSIE. Old lady's curtains.

KITTY. What old lady?

SUSIE. The one who lived here. The one who died here.

ELIZABETH. The famous Miss Aurora Chalmers.

KITTY. Famous? How?

ELIZABETH. Famous in her day, quite forgotten now. She had an extraordinary life – flew solo across the Channel at the age of eighteen, climbed Mont Blanc, nearly married a German count. Ended up writing dreadful novels, *On the Wilder Shores of Love*, *The Abandoned Heart*, *The Path of Passion*. This was the family home, the Chalmers family owned the whole house.

KITTY. God, is that the time?

ELIZABETH. There was a displenishment sale. I bought some of her things.

SUSIE. Displenishment. I always think that sounds like such a sad word.

ELIZABETH. She had no relatives, no one. No one who even wanted her things.

KITTY. You wanted her curtains.

SUSIE. Maybe she died in this room. Maybe she died right here. On this sofa. Everyone's got to die somewhere, after all.

ELIZABETH. That's my sofa, I brought it from the old flat. No one's died on it.

KITTY. Not yet.

SUSIE. Do you believe in ghosts?

ELIZABETH. I don't know.

SUSIE. I do.

KITTY. Listen to the pair of you. You're like a couple of old witches.

SUSIE. I always wanted to be a witch.

KITTY. And you are, Susie, you are, trust me.

SUSIE. I've never seen these photographs before. Are they the old lady's too? Miss Aurora Chalmers.

ELIZABETH. There was a whole suitcase of them. Photographs are so odd, aren't they? All these people, lost to time.

KITTY. They look a bit like you. You could pretend they were your real family, seeing as you don't have one of your own.

ELIZABETH. But I have you, dearest sister, I have you.

SUSIE. We're all related by blood to everyone if you go back far enough.

KITTY. How far?

SUSIE. Adam and Eve.

KITTY. Before the Fall. (*To* ELIZABETH.) Imagine.

SUSIE (*to* ELIZABETH). *You* can die here. Who will you leave your things to? Kitty? (*Laughs.*)

ELIZABETH. Kitty's older than me.

KITTY. That doesn't mean I'll die before you. When she dies I'd like that French carriage clock she keeps in the bedroom.

SUSIE. She?

ELIZABETH. The cat's mother.

KITTY. You know who.

ELIZABETH. Mother. Try it. Mo-th-er.

SUSIE. How will you divide her things up without fighting? You could go around putting little stickers on them – red for Kitty, blue for Elizabeth.

KITTY. Stickers?

SUSIE. Little round ones. Like dots. You can get them in Office World.

KITTY. I like Office World.

SUSIE. All women like stationery shops. No one knows why. It's one of life's little mysteries.

KITTY. All women? Even lesbians?

ELIZABETH. I think it's because they give you the illusion that you can live an orderly life. That you can sort things and file them, index and catalogue and staple, write in different coloured inks.

KITTY. Narrow ruled with margins.

ELIZABETH. Cartridge paper. A4, A5.

SUSIE. As 3, 2 and 1.

ELIZABETH. Reams of foolscap and quarto.

KITTY. Quires of imperial.

ALL THREE. Yeah.

KITTY. We should have a toast. (*Opens the champagne.*) To Lizzie's new flat.

SUSIE. Home sweet home.

KITTY. It *is* lovely though. It's like the Winter Palace or something. How much did you have to pay in the end?

ELIZABETH. Enough.

KITTY. Or Gothic, maybe. Victorian Gothic. This used to be the drawing-room, I suppose. Imagine what this house was like before it was converted.

SUSIE. Imagine the upkeep, the servants . . .

KITTY. But they knew how to live in style.

SUSIE. The servants?

KITTY. Better than your last place certainly, that was so full of the past.

ELIZABETH. And what might have been?

KITTY. What's happened to your carpet?

ELIZABETH. I haven't put it down yet – there's a problem with some of the wood – dry rot, wet rot, something. The wood people looked at it.

SUSIE. The wood people?

KITTY. Like some kind of New Age tribe? How much did you pay?

ELIZABETH. A lot.

KITTY. Tell me.

ELIZABETH. No.

KITTY. You've got a dado rail, nice.

SUSIE. You sound like your mother.

KITTY. Don't be so insulting.

ELIZABETH. You're so irretrievably bourgeois underneath all that street-cred crap.

KITTY. Me?

ELIZABETH. Yes, you. There's probably a gene that you got from her, the genteel gene, the one that likes embroidered peg-bags and hand-knitted toilet roll covers. It'll out in the end, you'll see, you'll be walking along the street one day when you'll suddenly feel compelled to run into Frasers and buy an antimacassar.

KITTY. All I said was 'dado'.

ELIZABETH. That's all you needed to say.

SUSIE. I don't think Frasers sell antimacassars anymore.

KITTY (to SUSIE). Tell her. Tell her that some things aren't inherited. Tell her.

SUSIE. You're terrified of turning into your mother.

KITTY. No, actually, I think I'm more terrified of turning into my father. Go on. How much did you pay? God, you're so annoying. You only won't tell me because I want to know.

SUSIE. Are you going to buy somewhere of your own, Kitty, now that you've moved back up here?

ELIZABETH. The return of the native.

SUSIE. Or are you just going to keep on sleeping in other people's beds?

KITTY. Miaow.

SUSIE. Elizabeth said you were sacked in London.

KITTY. I'm a journalist, journalists spend their lives getting sacked. It's not a word that has the same meaning for you as it does for us.

SUSIE. How is the new job going?

KITTY. I think you're confusing yourself with someone who gives a shite, Susie.

SUSIE. Oops, so I am.

ELIZABETH. Two hundred and fifty.

KITTY. Two hundred and fifty? Thousand? That's a quarter of a million. My God, you must be minted.

SUSIE. Minted? Is that tabloid lingo?

KITTY. Where do you get that kind of money from anyway? Since when did historians earn so much?

ELIZABETH. I saved. Something you wouldn't know anything about.

KITTY. You're such a spinster.

ELIZABETH. I'm a divorcee. You're the spinster.

SUSIE. An old maid.

KITTY. You can talk, you're a fucking dyke. Sorry, I didn't mean that.

SUSIE. Yes you did.

KITTY. Yes, but I didn't mean to *say* it.

SUSIE. Is it because I'm a dyke that you don't like me?

ELIZABETH. It's nothing personal. She doesn't like me either.

SUSIE. You're her sister, she's not supposed to like you.

KITTY. It wouldn't bother me if you were doing it with sea otters, Susie.

SUSIE. Sea otters?

ELIZABETH. She's not really my sister.

KITTY. Yes I am. Let's not fight, Liz. (*The doorbell rings.*)

ELIZABETH. Are we fighting?

KITTY. Yes.

ELIZABETH *lets* CALLUM *in.*

CALLUM. Hi. Mrs McMichael?

KITTY. Mrs?

CALLUM. Ms.

ELIZABETH. Mrs, Miss, Ms. Whatever.

CALLUM. Sorry I'm late. I was hindered – there was a tree down on the road. Amazing weather out there.

ELIZABETH (*puzzled*). Are you? Late?

CALLUM. I've come to give you an estimate? Callum Innes?

SUSIE. The 'Woodperson'.

ELIZABETH. Of course. Sorry.

CALLUM. Nice place. Top stuff. A lot of books. Have you read them all? Are you a teacher? Wow, look at that old light. Sweet.

ELIZABETH. So . . . do you just want to have a look at the . . . wood and see what you think?

CALLUM. Sure. No problem.

KITTY. Aren't you going to introduce us?

ELIZABETH. No.

KITTY (*to* CALLUM). Would you like a drink?

CALLUM. Cool. Thanks.

ELIZABETH (*to* KITTY). Excuse me?

KITTY. What? (*To* CALLUM.) My sister doesn't think the servants should be treated as equals. This is my sister. This is her best friend, Susie. She's a lesbian so don't waste your time.

CALLUM. Servants?

SUSIE. Ignore her. She has a disease that stops her from growing up.

CALLUM. Really?

ELIZABETH. So . . . the . . . rot?

CALLUM. Right. (*Starts looking round.*) You wonder about these old places, don't you? The people who lived in them, what they did, what they thought. Were they just like you and me? Did they have the same worries, think about the same stuff?

KITTY. I can see you're a thinker, Callum.

CALLUM. For a builder, you mean? I've got Highers you know, I was thinking about going to uni, but then I just thought, ah fuck it. You know? Everyone does stuff because they think they're supposed to, as if there was this invisible set of rules, like the Ten Commandments or something. And it's all shite – you get a degree, you buy a suit, get a job, you get married, have kids.

KITTY. Not everyone.

CALLUM. Not that kids aren't great, they are, they're fantastic. I've got a kid. Finn.

KITTY. Finn! We had a dog called Finn. Lizzie – Finn – remember Finn? Remember Finn, Susie?

SUSIE. Border collie. Black and white. Blue eyes.

ELIZABETH. Best dog in the world.

KITTY. Yes, best dog in the world.

Silence.

CALLUM. But. Anyway. It doesn't have to be like that. I mean you can do what you want really.

ELIZABETH. No rules?

CALLUM. Well, I'm not an anarchist.

KITTY. What are you then?

CALLUM. Well, I'm more into, kind of, otherworld stuff.

KITTY. Otherworld? Dear God, isn't this world enough?

ELIZABETH. Otherworld? Through the looking-glass.

SUSIE. And into the wardrobe.

CALLUM. The wardrobe?

SUSIE. The world we cannot see.

CALLUM. Well, yeah. Like vision quests, spirit journeys – shamanism.

SUSIE. Shamanism?

CALLUM. Yeah. Like I think we all have a spirit animal, for example.

KITTY. And yours is, hmm, let me guess now – a wolf?

CALLUM. How did you know?

KITTY (*laughs*). Everybody wants to be the wolf, Callum.

CALLUM. I believe there's a spiritual world that's the reflection of this one. The spiritual world is . . . watching over us.

ELIZABETH. No one's watching us. That's the tragedy.

SUSIE. That's the freedom. The world's indifferent to us. When nothing means anything then everything means something.

ELIZABETH. But no meaning, no meaning at all.

KITTY. You think there *might* be a meaning to life? You *so* still want to be a Catholic, don't you?

ELIZABETH. Don't you? All that certainty. When you're on your deathbed you'll be first in the queue for extreme unction.

KITTY. Well, of course I will. So will you. That's the beauty of it.

SUSIE (*to* CALLUM). So how do you find the wolf in you?

CALLUM (*doubtful*). Do you really want to know?

SUSIE. Yes, really. I'm interested.

KITTY. Susie's a scientist as well as a lesbian.

CALLUM. Cool. Science is amazing. Fractals and stuff. Chaos theory. The butterfly thing.

ELIZABETH. Butterfly?

CALLUM. You know – the butterfly flaps its wings in the Amazonian jungle and there's a hurricane in China. All that stuff.

SUSIE. Deterministic Nonperiodic Flow. Sensitive dependence on initial conditions. The infinite complexity of non-linear dynamics.

KITTY (*to* CALLUM). Lesbians, eh?

SUSIE. A small disturbance in the normal order of things having far-reaching consequences.

CALLUM (*to* SUSIE). Chaos specialist, are you?

SUSIE. No, that's Kitty.

KITTY. Piss off. She's a geneticist.

SUSIE. I'm a cell biologist actually.

CALLUM. Geneticist. I can't say I approve of that.

SUSIE. Approve?

CALLUM. Yes, but it's interfering with nature, isn't it? Scientists playing God. 'Do you want a blue-eyed baby or a brown-eyed one, Mrs Smith?' All that stuff. It's not that I've got anything against genes.

SUSIE. How could you possibly have anything against genes?

KITTY. Genes R Us.

CALLUM. I mean okay, survival – the selfish gene, life will find a way and all that.

SUSIE. Life will find a way?

KITTY. He's quoting from 'Jurassic Park'. Aren't you? Aren't you?

CALLUM. Yes. But all that Dolly and Polly stuff . . . anyway I should . . . get on. (*Looks around again.*) Hmm.

ELIZABETH. 'Hmm' – is that bad? It sounds bad.

CALLUM. It's not good. You should sue the people who did your survey. Except they have all kinds of get-out clauses and lawyers watching their backs. You're not a lawyer, are you?

KITTY. Historian.

CALLUM. Yeah? I've never seen the point of studying history. It's just battles and dates and lists of kings and queens. It's . . . gone, hasn't it? It's like the only moment that matters is the moment you're in. There is nothing else.

ELIZABETH. But history is people, not dates and battles.

CALLUM. Hmm.

ELIZABETH. Hmm again?

CALLUM. Who did the work on this before?

ELIZABETH. I've no idea.

CALLUM. Their spurs must have been jangling from a mile off.

ELIZABETH. Sorry?

CALLUM. Cowboys. I'll look at the rest, shall I? Better safe than sorry.

ELIZABETH. You sound like my mother.

CALLUM *exits to the bedroom.*

SUSIE. I like your mother.

ELIZABETH. I don't know why.

SUSIE. Because she's not mine.

ELIZABETH. He fancies you.

SUSIE (*laughs*). I know. He's quite cute.

KITTY. I saw Gregor the other day.

ELIZABETH. Gregor?

KITTY. You were married to him, remember? He was with the new wife. They had a baby with them.

ELIZABETH. Who? Who had a baby with who?

KITTY. Whom, don't you think? Who had a baby with whom. Gregor and the new Gregor wife.

SUSIE. A baby? They have a baby?

KITTY. We must suppose it was theirs. Unless they kidnapped it. (*Pause.*) Or adopted it. (*To* SUSIE.) Shouldn't you be getting back to your girlfriend? You wouldn't want her getting the wrong idea about you and Elizabeth.

SUSIE. Jo? She has a name. You could use it. She's on call tonight.

KITTY (*to* ELIZABETH). We have to fix a date for her. She wants to see your flat, I said I'd bring her over. Lunch or something.

CALLUM *enters.*

CALLUM. Well, the bad news is that your roof's nail-sick, I think your ceiling's poisoned, you've got woodworm, dry rot, wet rot. I think you might even have death-watch beetle.

KITTY. It's like a horror film, isn't it?

ELIZABETH. And the good news?

CALLUM (*shrugs*). It can all be fixed, I suppose. Everything can be fixed if you're prepared to spend the money.

SUSIE. Not everything.

CALLUM. So shall I drop you off an estimate or what? I'll be much cheaper than anyone else.

SUSIE. That's what they say about Kitty.

KITTY. I have to go. (*To* CALLUM.) Are you going? I'll show you to the door.

SUSIE. You can see it from here.

KITTY (*to* ELIZABETH). Come on give me a hug goodbye.

ELIZABETH. Hug?

They embrace awkwardly.

KITTY. God, what are you like?

Exit KITTY *and* CALLUM. *Darkness.*

ELIZABETH. Oh my God. What happened?

SUSIE. Spooky. (*Looks out of the window.*) The whole street's off.

Thunder and lightning. AGNES *walks across the back of the set.* ELIZABETH *lights a candle.*

ELIZABETH. I think I would like to have lived by candlelight. Sometimes don't you feel as if you could just reach out and . . . touch the past. I think people's lives somehow imprint themselves on houses.

SUSIE. Yeah, I know what you mean.

ELIZABETH. Not all people, not all houses. Maybe it's just when people have led dramatic lives. Passionate, eventful lives. Not like ours. Well, not like mine anyway. Sometimes I think you really could die of boredom.

SUSIE. Lizzie . . .

ELIZABETH. Perhaps they could put that on my death certificate – Elizabeth Jane McMichael, cause of death, extreme boredom. That sounds like a Hollywood movie, doesn't it? 'Coming soon – "Extreme Boredom" starring Arnold Schwarzenegger' –

SUSIE. Lizzie . . .

ELIZABETH. Sometimes I feel like a ghost inhabiting my own life, as if –

SUSIE. Elizabeth.

ELIZABETH. Sorry. What? (*Pause.*) What?

SUSIE. This might not be the best moment to tell you this. We've decided to try and have a baby.

ELIZABETH. We?

SUSIE. Jo and I.

ELIZABETH. A baby? (*Pause.*) You've never talked about wanting a baby.

SUSIE. I'm talking about it now.

ELIZABETH. Who's going to have it?

SUSIE. It?

ELIZABETH. The baby. You or Jo?

SUSIE. Me, I think. I hope. Jo works longer hours than me and plus she's a doctor and doctors aren't the most nurturing of people really, are they?

ELIZABETH. But she's younger than you are. Don't you feel you're too old?

SUSIE. I'm the same age as you.

ELIZABETH. Exactly.

SUSIE. You feel you're too old to have a baby? You've never said that.

ELIZABETH. I'm saying it now. (*Pause.*) How? A donor?

SUSIE. Well, yes. Anonymous donor. I think Jo would like it all to be controlled – a bit like Callum and his 'do you want a blue-eyed baby or a brown-eyed one'. Jo would probably go for the rocket scientist or concert pianist option.

ELIZABETH. That's what she'd like?

SUSIE. She likes the idea of perfection.

ELIZABETH. And you don't?

SUSIE. That's not Mother Nature's way is it? If life was perfect we'd be extinct. No adaptation, no selection, no change.

ELIZABETH. So you're going to take pot luck?

SUSIE. Well, half of the baby's genes will be mine. It'll be my baby. You're having a problem with this, aren't you?

ELIZABETH. No. Yes. Maybe. I don't know. (*Pause.*) It won't know who its father is.

SUSIE. Yes, but it'll know who its mother is, and anyway 'it' won't be the first. Every day people have sex with people they hardly know, complete strangers and – Bob's your uncle. Or your father. Or any Tom, Dick and Harry.

ELIZABETH. But that would leave it . . . incomplete. It'll spend its whole life wondering who it is. You know I died when I was born?

SUSIE. Well, enough about me and my life-changing decisions, why don't we talk about you?

ELIZABETH. What do you mean?

SUSIE. Maybe you should just move on with your life.

ELIZABETH. Move on? Where to?

Darkness.

Scene 2

A week later. ELIZABETH *setting the table etc.* CALLUM *working.*

CALLUM. You're entertaining.

ELIZABETH. I am – laugh a minute.

CALLUM. No, I meant you're entertaining . . . guests.

ELIZABETH. I know, I know that's what you meant.

CALLUM. I should make myself scarce.

ELIZABETH. I wouldn't bother. It's only my mother.

CALLUM. You're not married then? Haven't got anyone steady?

ELIZABETH. You can tell that by looking at me?

CALLUM. Nah, it's just, you know, there's no trace of a guy around the place.

ELIZABETH. You haven't found spoor or droppings?

CALLUM. I thought you might be . . .

ELIZABETH. Gay?

CALLUM. Hey, gay's cool, doesn't worry me. Or not gay, that's cool too. If you are, if you're not . . . whatever turns you on, as they say, that's my philosophy.

ELIZABETH. What if Finn was gay?

CALLUM. He's only three. He's a fucking brilliant kid. I've spent so much time with him since he was born. I think I've spent more time with him than Laura has.

ELIZABETH. Laura?

CALLUM. My girlfriend. She's great. We're solid, you know? Do you want to see a photograph of Finn?

ELIZABETH. He's a lovely boy.

CALLUM. I don't think he's gay. Do you?

The doorbell rings.

ELIZABETH. Oh God, she's here.

Exit CALLUM *to bedroom.* ELIZABETH *answers the door,* INA *comes in followed by* KITTY.

INA. I think it's going to snow.

ELIZABETH (*to* KITTY). You're early.

KITTY. Well, look at it this way – the sooner she comes the sooner she goes.

ELIZABETH. It doesn't work like that, as well you know.

INA. What are you two whispering about?

ELIZABETH. Nothing.

INA. So here you are then. Let me have a look at you. You've put on weight. Wasn't that nice of Kitty, coming and getting me in the car like that? Of course, we're lucky to be alive the way your sister drives, she certainly plays fast and loose with the highway code. I could have got the bus, it's not as if I live that far away, but you never know if they're going to be running to timetable, do you? I went to the doctor's yesterday and I had to wait nearly an hour on a 12. In the rain. It's very difficult when you have to do these things on your own. With no one to help you. (*To* KITTY.) You can ask me why I went to the doctor's.

ELIZABETH. No, I haven't.

INA. No you haven't what?

ELIZABETH. Put on weight.

KITTY. Maybe just a little bit.

ELIZABETH. I have not.

INA. Now girls, don't fight.

KITTY. We're not fighting.

INA. Sounds like it to me. You did nothing but fight as children. I always wished you were more like Susan, she never fought.

ELIZABETH. Susie's an only child.

INA. She was always very well-behaved, she still is. So . . . this is your new flat, Elizabeth, very . . . antique. You've not got much of a view, have you? How much did it cost?

ELIZABETH (*deadpan*). A hundred thousand.

INA (*gasps dramatically*). A hundred thousand!

KITTY *raises her eyebrows and mouths 'A hundred thousand?' at* ELIZABETH.

ELIZABETH. I'm minted, didn't you know?

INA. A hundred thousand – I don't know how you dare. Let's hope you don't lose your job.

ELIZABETH. Why would I lose my job?

INA. Well you never know these days, look at Kitty, she lost hers.

ELIZABETH. She was sacked.

INA (*to* KITTY). You were never!

KITTY (*to* ELIZABETH). Thanks. (*To* INA.) Of course, I wasn't.

ELIZABETH. Weren't you?

INA. Well, never mind, she's got another one now. (*To* KITTY). I like that new paper you're working for, it's much easier to read than the last one, smaller, much better stories. Human interest, that's what they call it, isn't it?

ELIZABETH. I call it the gutter press.

INA. Is it just me or is there a funny smell in here?

KITTY. It's just you.

INA *gets up and wanders around the room.*

INA. It looks like you're ready to have a séance. You have such old-fashioned taste. This stuff just gathers dust. And you don't know where any of it's been. It's all things that no one else wants anymore. Just because you write about history doesn't mean you have to live with it.

KITTY. Yes, you should try going to Ikea, buying new for once.

INA. Look at all these photographs. Who on earth are they?

ELIZABETH. Nobody.

INA. Nobody? You can't have a photograph of nobody, they'd be invisible, it would be just . . . background. Hedges and trees and empty beaches. This isn't our family.

ELIZABETH. They were left in the house. By the old lady who used to live here.

INA. So you have photographs of dead people – of complete strangers – and you don't have any of your own family? Of me and Daddy? Where are we? That's a funny colour for curtains, what would you call that, sort of slime green?

KITTY. Chartreuse.

INA. Daddy always used to say don't drink anything alcoholic unless it's brown.

ELIZABETH. Sorry?

INA. Sherry, whisky, Guinness. I like a glass of Guinness. It does you good. That's what they say. And they're right.

ELIZABETH. I can give you a sherry. I've got sherry. Or gin.

KITTY (to INA). You like a drop of gin.

INA. A wee drappy.

ELIZABETH. Gin doesn't really have a colour, does it? But then everything must have a colour, surely? Or does everything have no colour at all?

KITTY. White, I think. I think everything's white.

INA. White? Everything's white? You're not colour blind are you? Surely you'd have noticed before now. Do albinos see everything in white? It's a shame Susan isn't here. She'd be able to tell us.

ELIZABETH. Sherry, sherry then. Kitty?

KITTY. Just give me a shot of the waters of Lethe then. Straight up.

INA. The water of Leith? I wouldn't drink that.

KITTY. I think white is composed of all the colours of the rainbow.

INA. She was wonderful. *Meet me in St Louis*, *A Star is Born*, *The Wizard of Oz*, I'm melting, I'm melting!

KITTY. There's no place like home.

INA. Oh, you've got a dado rail. Lovely. Aren't you going to have a carpet down on this floor? Or are you going to keep the bare boards? That's very fashionable, you know. You can paint them, I saw it on Richard and Judy.

KITTY. There's a problem with the floor.

INA. Problem? What kind of problem?

KITTY. Rot.

INA. Rot?

ELIZABETH. It's fine.

INA. You can't cope with that kind of thing on your own.

ELIZABETH. Why not?

INA. You need a man for that kind of thing. When are you going to find someone else, Elizabeth? Everyone needs someone. Someone to watch over them. Do you know how much it worries me? It's terrible on your own. I would give anything to have Daddy back.

KITTY. Dad? Why would you want him back?

INA. Because he was my husband.

ELIZABETH. But he was horrible to you.

INA. What a dreadful thing to say.

ELIZABETH. But it's true.

KITTY. He hit you. Will you never admit it?

INA. Don't change the subject, I was talking about you. You're forty-one years old, when are you going to find someone else?

KITTY. Maybe when you've lost weight.

ELIZABETH. Fuck off.

INA. Elizabeth! Wash your mouth out.

ELIZABETH. I'm not forty-one yet.

INA. Oh, excuse me, forty years, ten months and . . .

KITTY. Sixteen days.

INA. Thank you, Katherine.

ELIZABETH. Thank you, Katherine.

INA. Two daughters and neither of them mothers, it's not natural. (*To* ELIZABETH.) Everything would have been different if you'd had children with Gregor.

ELIZABETH. No it wouldn't.

INA. Yes it would. Children bind you to a marriage.

KITTY. Is that why you stayed with Dad? Because of us?

INA. Maybe you're barren.

ELIZABETH. Barren?

KITTY. Why don't we eat now? Everything looks lovely.

INA (*to* KITTY). You're even older.

KITTY. Thanks.

INA. It's getting very late for Mother Nature to come knocking on your door. You must be down to the last egg in the carton by now, your biological alarm clock should be ringing very loudly.

KITTY. My what?

INA. Your biological alarm clock.

ELIZABETH (*laughing*). She probably read about it in your paper.

KITTY. I'm only forty-one

INA *and* ELIZABETH. Forty-two.

INA. Are you going to settle down and give me grandchildren?

KITTY. Me? I hate kids, I'm never having any.

INA. How can you say hate children?

KITTY. I hate children, I hate children, I hate children. It's easy. Try it. It should come naturally to you.

INA. Women were made to have babies. You may both be very clever, I know you're both very clever and I know I'm very stupid (*Holds up her hand to stop them contradicting her, neither of them make a move.*) no, I know I'm a stupid old woman who doesn't have Highers and degrees and careers and I've never burnt my bra –

KITTY. Oh for Christ's sake –

ELIZABETH. Wash your mouth out, Katherine.

INA. All I'm saying is that it would be nice if both of you had a man.

ELIZABETH. The same one?

INA. Don't be silly. You can make fun, but one day you're going to be old women and all alone in the world.

KITTY. Like you.

INA. I'm a widow, that's different. You never introduce me to any of your young men.

ELIZABETH. Introduce? I bet you can't name the last man you slept with.

KITTY. . . .

INA. Anyway, there's more to love than sex.

KITTY. There's more to sex than love.

INA. I never enjoyed the physical side of love, nonetheless, Daddy and I –

CALLUM *enters from the bedroom.*

INA. Goodness, you've got a man in your bedroom, Elizabeth.

KITTY. A man with a tool.

ELIZABETH. This is Callum.

KITTY. The woodperson.

CALLUM. I'd better get going,

INA. You can't leave before you've been introduced.

ELIZABETH. Callum, this is my mother, mother, this is Callum. Goodbye, Callum.

INA. I remember when she called me 'Mummy'. She was such an affectionate child. And now look at her.

KITTY. Was I an affectionate child?

INA (*doubtfully*). You?

KITTY. Yes. Me.

INA. Elizabeth was mummy's little helper. Daddy, my husband, had his own business, he did very well. The girls wanted for nothing. Daddy was highly thought of in the business community. The turnout for his funeral was wonderful. He was a self-made man, you know. Born into the gutter. Rose to be a local councillor.

KITTY (*to* ELIZABETH). Could you please stop her?

ELIZABETH. Me? You think I can stop her?

CALLUM. I really should go.

INA. Oh, don't go. Why don't you stay and eat with us?

ELIZABETH (*to* INA). I'm sorry?

KITTY. Eating with the servants.

INA. It'll be nice to have the company of a man.

KITTY. Yes, you can be our token man. No, better still you can pretend to be one of the family. She always wanted a son.

CALLUM. Is that okay, Liz?

They all sit down at the table.

INA (*shivering*). Oh, there's a draught over here. Isn't this lovely, all of us back round the one table again? I'm so glad you moved back, Kitty. Girls shouldn't live a long way away from their mother. And London's no place to live. There's nothing with anything spicy in it, is there? Kitty made me eat a chicken tikka mascara or whatever it's called and it went straight through me. Or garlic in? (*To* CALLUM.) I have a hiatus hernia.

KITTY. *An* hiatus hernia perhaps.

INA. An hiatus hernia? That sounds silly.

KITTY. Not like anything else you say then?

INA (*to* CALLUM). I can't hear anything she says if she speaks into that ear.

CALLUM (*shouting*). Are you deaf in that ear?

INA. No.

KITTY. What is that exactly? Hiatus hernia – I've never understood.

INA. It's a nightmare, that's what it is. Oh, guess who's dead?

KITTY. Oh, I love that game.

ELIZABETH. Who?

INA. Mr Scrymegour, that lived next door to me. One minute as right as rain, the next dead behind the toilet door. (*To* CALLUM.) He was what we used to call a confirmed bachelor.

CALLUM. Oh?

INA. A pansy. A fairy. (*Mouths to* CALLUM.) Homosexual.

CALLUM. Gay.

INA. Nothing very gay about Mr Scrymegour.

KITTY. Not now, that's for sure.

CALLUM. Gay's cool. I wouldn't mind being gay. I'd quite like to be gay.

INA. Oh dear.

ELIZABETH (*to* KITTY). Do you want to open that wine?

INA. Oh, that's a man's job, give it to Callum to open.

KITTY. It's red.

INA. What is?

KITTY. The wine.

INA. I can see that.

KITTY. It's not brown.

INA. What are you talking about? Brown wine? Whoever heard of such a thing? Or herbs. I can't handle herbs.

ELIZABETH. I cooked a chicken, a very plain chicken.

INA. Isn't there a rule about red wine and white meat?

ELIZABETH. I really don't think it matters.

KITTY. I don't think there are any rules any more.

CALLUM. I'm a vegetarian.

KITTY. What a surprise.

INA. You have to have rules.

KITTY. Why?

CALLUM. It's okay, I'll just eat the vegetables.

INA. Nobody would know what they were doing if there weren't any rules.

KITTY. Nobody knows what they're doing anyway.

INA. Queen for a day.

CALLUM. Sorry?

INA. Elizabeth and Susan were always playing that. You had your own little kingdom and you made up all the rules. You used to really love that, Elizabeth.

KITTY. I bet you did. (*To* ELIZABETH, *laughing*.) You did like it a lot. You were always Queen. Susie was always your servant.

INA. Happy days.

KITTY (*to* ELIZABETH). Is she being ironic?

ELIZABETH. I don't think she knows the meaning of the word.

INA. Susie's a scientist now, you know, Callum. I don't understand any of it. Dolly. Is that something to do with her. Making sheep.

KITTY. She knits them.

INA. Hello Dolly.

ELIZABETH. I don't think that's what Susie does.

INA. Who was that? Barbra Streisand? Since my operation food just goes straight through me. (*To* CALLUM.) Of course, I've never been really right since Kitty was born.

ELIZABETH. Please. We're eating.

INA (*whispers loudly*). She brought everything out with her.

ELIZABETH. *Please.*

INA. Well it wasn't very nice for me either. (*Leans over and touches* CALLUM*'s hand.*) Callum doesn't mind, do you Callum? That's why we adopted Elizabeth because I couldn't have any more of my own.

KITTY. I'm the real daughter.

INA. Kitty, that's not very nice.

KITTY. I know.

CALLUM (*to* ELIZABETH). You're adopted?

KITTY. Can't you tell?

CALLUM. Tell? How do you tell?

INA. Elizabeth was an abandoned baby.

CALLUM. Really?

INA. In a public toilet. A gentleman's public toilet. At night. In February. In the snow. Left to die. In a paper bag.

CALLUM. A paper bag?

INA. Well, quite a big one. A carrier more like.

KITTY. A bag baby.

INA. It's not like being left in a handbag in the Ladies in Jenners is it?

CALLUM. A handbag?

KITTY. Don't even go there.

INA. A foundling.

ELIZABETH. Can we just drop this subject, please?

INA. And it *was* just mere chance that someone came by. The man who found her said he'd been celebrating a friend's birthday so he'd had a couple pints more than usual, so he needed, you know . . .

CALLUM. A slash.

INA. Of course, it's surprising he went into a convenience at all, most men just take it out anywhere.

CALLUM. You see – the butterfly effect – just a small change – an extra pint of beer – and a huge consequence – you don't die.

INA. She was double-wrapped, I suppose somebody was thinking about her welfare.

CALLUM. Double-wrapped?

INA. In newspaper.

KITTY. Like a fish supper. A single fish.

CALLUM. Like a gift.

ELIZABETH. Thank you.

INA. She'd actually stopped breathing.

ELIZABETH. Dead. I was dead. I was brought back from the dead.

INA. They had to give her the kiss of life. They were worried she might be brain-damaged.

KITTY. And was she?

INA. They kept everything, the welfare people, the bag, the newspaper.

ELIZABETH (*to* INA). It's very important. Every scrap is important when you have so little.

INA. The ink from the newspaper was on her skin, like a tattoo. Letters and bits of words, smudges and blots. Only one whole word.

CALLUM. What word?

INA. Retriever.

CALLUM. Retriever? Retrieve her? Cool.

KITTY. It was an article about the Kennel Club.

CALLUM (*to* ELIZABETH). Have you never tried to trace your real mother?

INA. She can't trace her real mother. How could she?

ELIZABETH. There's no way, no birth certificate, nothing.

KITTY. You used to love all those fairy stories about blue-blooded girls who ended up living the wrong life as a servant.

CALLUM. Cinderella.

ELIZABETH. Snow-White, the Goose Girl.

KITTY. You were convinced you were a princess in disguise. You still are.

INA. I wasn't going to tell her she was adopted, of course.

ELIZABETH. Never?

INA. But then Kitty –

KITTY. I told her on her tenth birthday. She broke one of my skates. I was so annoyed.

ELIZABETH. You just came right out with it, 'You were left on a doorstep, no one wanted you.'

INA. What a terrible thing to say.

KITTY. It was true.

ELIZABETH. It wasn't a doorstep.

INA. They've fought like cat and dog ever since they were little. Kitty was so jealous of Elizabeth when we first brought her home. Put a pillow over her face the first week. Dropped her on her head the second week.

KITTY. Happy days.

INA. Cuckoo in the nest. That's what the psychiatrist said. That there was a cuckoo in Kitty's nest.

ELIZABETH (*to* KITTY). Psychiatrist? I thought you didn't see a psychiatrist until after your suicide.

CALLUM. Suicide?

INA. Don't be silly. Look at that snow.

KITTY. Attempted suicide obviously. I'm still here.

ELIZABETH. Silly?

INA. I think we should have a toast to Elizabeth's new home.

CALLUM (*raising his glass*). How about to . . . the future.

ELIZABETH. And the past, let's not forget the past.

AGNES *enters. Everyone else gets up and starts to clear the table.*

CALLUM. I really should go now. My girlfriend will be wondering where I am. Lovely to meet you, Mrs McMichael.

INA. Oh Callum, goodbye then.

CALLUM *exits.*

ELIZABETH (*to* INA). You'll need to be getting home soon I expect.

INA. Will I?

ELIZABETH *exits to the kitchen.*

INA. Look at that blizzard.

KITTY. The thing is you didn't choose me, did you?

INA. You know how to drive in snow, do you?

KITTY. No.

INA. Are you joking? (*Pause.*) You are, aren't you?

KITTY. You *had* me but you didn't *choose* me. You chose
Elizabeth. You said, 'I'll have that one, please'.

INA. I didn't. I didn't say that.

KITTY. What did you say then?

INA. I have no idea. I probably said, this one will make a nice
sister for our little Kitty.

KITTY. No you didn't. (*Pause.*) I wasn't enough.

INA. Daddy wanted two children.

KITTY. And what did you want?

INA. A happy family.

KITTY. Missed out there then, didn't you? (*Walks over to
the window.*) I love it when it snows. It's as if the earth is
being wrapped in a shawl and put to bed. Everything
peaceful, everything white. You can imagine that when
the world wakes up again it will have been cleansed of all
its badness.

Exit INA *to kitchen, enter* ELIZABETH.

ELIZABETH. What?

KITTY. Nothing. What do you think's the last colour you see
when you die?

ELIZABETH. White? Isn't that what people who have near
death experiences see, bright white lights and all that.

KITTY. You died. You're forever going on about it. What
colour was it for you?

ELIZABETH. I was only a few hours old. Don't you
remember, when you overdosed?

KITTY. I only remember blackness. Endless night. Do you
think there ever was a time when all people on earth were
happy? A golden age, a state of grace from which we've
fallen?

ELIZABETH. No, I think we've always been fucked up.

Enter INA.

INA. Well, it makes a change to see you having a pleasant conversation for once.

KITTY. As long as it isn't chartreuse.

INA. What?

KITTY. The colour of death.

INA. Are you all right?

KITTY. Me? Top of the world, ma. Top of the world.

Scene 3

Later that evening. ELIZABETH *reading a copy of 'The List'. A knock on the door.*

KITTY. Drink, give me a drink.

Enter KITTY.

ELIZABETH. You drink too much.

KITTY. You don't drink enough. And anyway you've not just driven Judy Garland home to the Land of Oz.

KITTY *reads from 'The List'.*

KITTY. What about a film? There's nothing on. What about a play?

ELIZABETH. It's still snowing.

KITTY. 'The Three Sisters' is on. I hate Chekhov. They're all so passive. Always looking back, so nostalgic all the time – do you remember blah, blah, blah. Moscow, Moscow, if only we were in Moscow, if only our cherry orchard wasn't being chopped down.

ELIZABETH. You're like that.

KITTY. I am not.

ELIZABETH. Yes you are. London, London, if only I was back in London. Blah, blah, blah.

KITTY. That's a load of shite.

ELIZABETH. The Two Sisters. 'Blood Brothers' – can that still be on?

KITTY. Blood Sisters. They don't say that, do they? (*Doubtful*.) Do they?

ELIZABETH. No. It's all musicals.

KITTY. 'The Three Sisters' isn't a musical. It would be better if it was.

ELIZABETH. 'I saw you'.

KITTY. I like that.

ELIZABETH. That's because you have a narcissistic personality disorder.

KITTY. I do not.

ELIZABETH. Do. Right, so what are we looking for – 'I saw you, you promiscuous tabloid hack – or should that be hackette – with silly little backpack, no morals and a speech impediment'.

KITTY. What speech impediment?

ELIZABETH. Say mother.

KITTY. M . . . nah, can't do it.

ELIZABETH. You're not in here. Nobody's spotted your talents. Nobody's fallen in love with you at first sight.

KITTY. I don't want someone falling in love with me.

ELIZABETH. You do really. You do.

KITTY. I don't. Being in love's like . . . being mad. Or ill. You lose control. You lose control of your . . . self.

ELIZABETH. You make it sound like diarrhoea.

KITTY. You'd like to fall in love again.

ELIZABETH. Well, yes I would actually. I would like someone to cherish me. I don't want to spend the rest of my life on my own, I don't see what's wrong with that.

KITTY. You don't have to be defensive with me.

ELIZABETH. At least when you're in love you're not bored.

KITTY. Speak for yourself.

ELIZABETH. This isn't how I intended my life to turn out. I thought I'd be with Gregor forever.

KITTY. How poetic. Gregor forever. Like a cheap tattoo. If I was going to be in love it would have to be with someone who understood me. Completely. In the way I understand myself. Like . . . an identical twin.

ELIZABETH. Maybe you could get cloned. If I was loved it would make me feel . . . safe.

KITTY. Safe from what?

ELIZABETH. Everything. The way God would do – if you still believed in him.

KITTY. Which would be nice but ridiculous.

ELIZABETH. Or the perfect mother.

KITTY. Which would be nice but ridiculous.

ELIZABETH. Safe from death I suppose.

KITTY. I'm not afraid of dying.

ELIZABETH. I know, you tried to kill yourself.

KITTY. Everybody misinterpreted that.

ELIZABETH. Misinterpreted? You drank a bottle of vodka and swallowed half a bottle of her sleeping pills.

KITTY. I was only fourteen, for Christ's sake. It doesn't count.

ELIZABETH. It would have counted if you'd succeeded.

KITTY. Well, I didn't. (*Pause.*) I don't know what I was thinking, it was a long time ago. I suppose I was thinking 'maybe someone will take some notice of me now'.

ELIZABETH. I can't imagine being dead. Annihilation. Just to . . . to not *be*. Not to exist. How can the self be obliterated? How can that be? When we are so . . . alive.

How can all of this be for no reason? Except for what – to hand on little packets of genes. Forever and forever until the sun destroys our planet. And then what, time goes on without us? Can time exist without an observer? Can time end?

KITTY. We really need to get out more. (*Pause.*) Lizzie?

ELIZABETH. What? You only call me that when you're after something.

KITTY. This is something for you not me.

ELIZABETH. Oh? What?

KITTY. I've been thinking . . .

ELIZABETH. Oh?

KITTY. Look, you're coming up to your birthday, right? So – it would be a good time, wouldn't it, to have another shot at finding your mother? Your real mother. It's an anniversary – you know the kind of thing, 'forty-one years ago today' – of course, it would have sounded better if it had been 'forty years ago' –

ELIZABETH. You're thinking in headlines.

KITTY. If she read it, it would give her an opportunity to come forward – if she knew you were looking for her, if she knew you wanted to see her. She must want to see you.

ELIZABETH. If she *read* it? You do mean a newspaper article, don't you? Splashed across your paper. My life, your copy. How could you? With your by-line, no doubt. I don't want to appear in your paper, its politics are disgusting, its morals are . . . tainted.

KITTY. It's not like that. Honestly. I'm trying to help you. Think about it – a big feature piece. It would be the best way of getting publicity, of jogging memories. We have a huge circulation.

ELIZABETH. What if she's a Guardian reader?

KITTY. I know how much it means to you. (*Pause.*) We could just go out for a drink.

ELIZABETH. I don't want to go out.

KITTY. Please think about it, Lizzie.

ELIZABETH. No, no way, definitely, absolutely not. No.

KITTY. You'll change your mind. You know you will.

Darkness. Enter AGNES. *Lights go up,* ELIZABETH, *and* KITTY *in same positions as before.*

ELIZABETH (*reluctantly*). Okay, I'll do it.

Darkness.

Scene 4

AGNES. Blah. Blah. Blah. Blah, blah, blah. Bob's your uncle. Tom, Dick and Harry. Dolly, Polly. Dolly, Polly, Holly, Golly, Brolly, Jolly. Jolly good show. Folly. The height of. Dead as a dado. Dede as a deado. Dode as a . . . no. I-key-a. Forever and forever and forever, amen. Forever and forever and forever and forever and forever . . .

Chartreuse, retriever, narrow ruled with margins. I do not seem to know the lingo. Sea otters. I am a creature of fragments and tatters. A piece of shoddy. What a shoddy piece of work is woman. Minted. I am new minted. No, I am old coin, clipped and abused. What am I? What woeful world of half-formed shadows am I inhabiting? What kind of wretched creature am I? There is no God in heaven and all is wrong with the world. Can no one help me? This is not how I expected my life to turn out.

Scene 5

A week later.

CALLUM *working,* SUSIE *watching.*

CALLUM. Maybe we're not meant to understand the workings of every last molecule and atom and . . . whatever's smaller than an atom.

SUSIE. Electrons, neutrons and protons. Molecules are quite big in the scheme of things.

CALLUM. They're not so big you can see them.

SUSIE. So, if we can't see something we shouldn't study it? Anything smaller than a small flea is consigned to mystery? I thought it was the world you couldn't see that attracted you.

CALLUM. That's different.

SUSIE. How?

CALLUM. What I'm trying to say is . . . if you analyse and dissect then you destroy the whole.

SUSIE. The world we can't see is fantastic and as mysterious in its own way as the realm of angels or your Celtic otherworld. And because we know how things work doesn't make them less precious or less wonderful. The butterfly is still the most gloriously beautiful creature, even though –

CALLUM. But if we were supposed to understand the minute workings of everything, then why weren't we born with that knowledge?

SUSIE. We were born with the ability to *acquire* it. With brains that could invent light microscopes and ask why the giraffe has a long neck and how can brown-eyed parents have blue-eyed children. There's no point in being some kind of evolutionary Luddite. As a species we've been given the possibility of evolving into our most advanced *idea* of ourselves.

CALLUM. Did I show you a photo of Finn?

SUSIE. Nice, really – he looks like a lovely wee boy.

CALLUM. Is it difficult being gay?

SUSIE. Are you sure she said she wasn't going to be long?

CALLUM. She said she was just popping out. I've got to go soon. I've got to pick Finn up from nursery school and give him his tea. (*Enter* ELIZABETH.) Here she is.

ELIZABETH. What? Have I been missed? (*Kisses* SUSIE.) Hi.

SUSIE. God, you're freezing.

ELIZABETH. Sleet. The worst kind of weather. Sleet. Even the word makes me feel cold.

CALLUM (*to* ELIZABETH). I was going to say to you. I was thinking of taking some time off next week.

ELIZABETH. You've only been working here a few days.

CALLUM. Yeah, but there's this sort of pagan festival. Up north. And . . . I wanted to go, take Finn.

ELIZABETH. Finn?

SUSIE. His son.

CALLUM (*to* SUSIE). Don't you think we've lost something. Don't you think we're cut off from nature, from the seasons, the phases of the moon, the stars, the weather?

ELIZABETH. I don't feel cut off from the weather.

CALLUM. We need to look at hills and trees and wonder at the night sky.

SUSIE. I agree, we do.

CALLUM. And feel the . . . vastness of . . .

SUSIE. Creation?

ELIZABETH. Don't let me interrupt anything.

CALLUM. The mystery of . . . everything and the . . . our . . .

SUSIE. Soul?

CALLUM. Yeah.

ELIZABETH. Is this part of your hourly rate? Just out of curiosity?

CALLUM. Sorry. (*Exits to bedroom.*)

ELIZABETH. Are you teasing him?

SUSIE. No, not at all. I like him. He's sweet. He may not believe in molecules but he believes in love and childcare and world peace. One could do worse.

ELIZABETH. One could do better. How are you?

SUSIE. Okay.

ELIZABETH. How's the getting pregnant thing?

SUSIE. The getting pregnant thing is . . . not really happening.
No one's actually pregnant yet. All this counselling and
stuff at the clinic, it's all so, I don't know, *clinical*. It feels
stupid. There seems to be a lot of talking involved in getting
pregnant.

ELIZABETH. I'm sure my mother managed it without saying
a word.

SUSIE. Which one?

ELIZABETH. Which word?

SUSIE. Which mother. Which mother are we talking about
now?

ELIZABETH. Ina. The unreal one. But funny you should
mention that.

SUSIE. What?

ELIZABETH. Kitty.

SUSIE. The most common synonym for trouble.

ELIZABETH. Kitty wants to write an article for her paper
about my . . . abandonment. She thinks that's my only
chance now of ever finding her. My birth mother. My own
version of the anonymous donor.

SUSIE. She's probably right.

ELIZABETH. I know. That's the really annoying thing. I
imagine it all the time. How it was. My . . . mother. She was
probably just a terrified schoolgirl. She might not have told
anyone about it. Ever. She might have carried the guilt around
all this time. Had sex with some boy, pretended she wasn't
pregnant – probably pretended to herself more than anyone –
and then when it happened, she just . . . had to get rid of it.

SUSIE. It?

ELIZABETH. Me. She must want to meet me really.

SUSIE. Must she?

ELIZABETH. Of course. I have to go out again. Did you want something? Or did you just drop in for a chat?

SUSIE. Oh, you know, just a chat.

ELIZABETH. Another time then? It'll keep?

SUSIE. Sure, it'll keep.

Exit ELIZABETH, *enter* CALLUM

CALLUM. Has she gone? What're you doing?

SUSIE. Rolling a joint.

CALLUM. Cool. Didn't take you for a smoker.

SUSIE. Are you happy?

CALLUM. Dunno. Most of the time. Are you?

SUSIE. I thought I was.

CALLUM. And now you don't? It's nothing to do with being gay or anything?

SUSIE. No I think it's just to do with being me. I want a baby. I really want a baby. I hadn't even realised how much until we started all this. I want a baby. I want a baby. I want a fucking baby.

CALLUM. I'll help you out, if you want.

SUSIE. That is very kind of you, Callum, but no thanks.

Darkness.

Scene 6

A few days later ELIZABETH *is working,* AGNES *wanders around listlessly. The doorbell rings,* ELIZABETH *answers it.* ALEC *stands on the doorstep, carrying a lot of photographic equipment*

ALEC. I thought there was no one in for a minute. People are always out at the weekend.

ELIZABETH. I'm not. Why did you come if you thought I was going to be out?

ALEC. I didn't think you would be, I thought you might be. Alec, Alec Frazer. Your sister asked me to come? She's doing an article about you for the paper? I saw her this morning and she asked me to take some photographs. I owe her a favour, so . . .

ELIZABETH. And I thought you were just carrying that lot around for fun. You'd better come in.

ALEC. You don't sound very keen.

ELIZABETH. Sorry. I'm just . . .

ALEC. I know, people hate having their photograph taken. It's going to take me a while to get set up. (*Starts setting up his equipment.*) You've got a lot of books. Have you read them all? Sometimes I think books –

ELIZABETH. What?

ALEC. Nothing.

ELIZABETH. Books what?

ALEC (*laughs*). Too many words.

ELIZABETH. Books have too many words?

ALEC. I'm more of a visuals man. I don't really think of a thing as real until I've photographed it. Maybe there's something wrong with me, I don't know. Are you a writer then?

ELIZABETH. No.

ALEC. A teacher?

ELIZABETH. I'm an historian.

ALEC. Must pay well.

ELIZABETH. I'm minted.

ALEC. Have I caught you at a bad moment?

ELIZABETH. No. I don't know. I'm sorry. I knew you were coming, I just forgot.

ALEC. That's okay. So what does an historian do exactly then?

ELIZABETH. Write books, articles. Give talks, lectures. That kind of thing.

ALEC. Great. Nearly there now. Do you live on your own?

ELIZABETH. Yes.

ALEC. It's a nice flat. Not even a cat?

ELIZABETH. A cat?

ALEC. I thought most single women had cats, isn't there some statistic? How more women have a cat than a partner?

ELIZABETH. I used to have a dog, but it died.

ALEC. That sounds like a bad joke.

ELIZABETH. I used to have a husband. He didn't die. He slept with someone else.

ALEC. I'm sorry.

ELIZABETH. With my sister.

ALEC. With your sister what?

ELIZABETH. He slept with my sister. My husband slept with my sister.

ALEC. Men are bastards, eh?

ELIZABETH. Not all of them.

ALEC. With Kitty? He slept with Kitty?

ELIZABETH. It's all in the past.

ALEC. I think women are much more, I don't know . . . sound, than men, more moral, more responsible. If I had the choice I'd rather be a woman.

ELIZABETH. Really?

ALEC. Yeah, really. Women are much better at . . . life. And love as well, men are really bad at that. This won't take long. I'll try and make it as painless as possible. You really look as if you're about to be tortured.

ELIZABETH. It's okay.

ALEC. You're not worried I'm about to steal your soul?

ELIZABETH. Steal my soul? What if that were possible? It's the only thing we have that we can truly call our own.

ALEC. Then it must be the only thing we can't lose. Are you a Catholic?

ELIZABETH. Can you tell by looking?

ALEC. Takes one to know one. Takes a lapsed one to know a lapsed one.

ELIZABETH. Do you think we have a soul? Really?

ALEC. I can almost see yours. Trust me. (*Pause.*) Do you want to sit on there, it's a nice light. Lovely big window. Can you put your chin down slightly. A bit more. But keep your eyes up. Look over my shoulder somewhere to the right a bit. That's good. Keep your chin down. Do you think you can smile?

ELIZABETH. At what?

ALEC. Maybe not. Would you like to turn this way a bit? No, like this. (*Goes over to her and moves her into the right position.*) What's this piece about? It's okay, you don't have to tell me.

ELIZABETH. No, it's not that, it's . . . it's about how I was found. Well, about how I was lost. I was lost and then I was found.

ALEC. Now that sounds like a religious thing.

ELIZABETH. I was abandoned when I was a baby. When I was born.

ALEC. Jesus, that's dreadful. That must really do things to your head – not knowing who your parents are, you must feel a part of yourself is missing.

ELIZABETH. Yes. And it runs through you all the time, like an infection in the blood. You feel, I don't know, that there must be something wrong with you, that even when you were a few hours old, there was something about you . . .

there was something so bad about you . . . that you had to be got rid of.

ALEC. Even though you know it's not true.

ELIZABETH. But do I really know that?

ALEC. Yes, of course. Because when you were born you were completely innocent. Completely. Absolutely. No stains on your soul, no blots on your copybook, just a brand new person who deserved all the treasures in the world heaped around her cradle and instead you ended up paying for, I don't know, original sin.

ELIZABETH. Would you like a cup of coffee?

ALEC. Coffee?

ELIZABETH. Or anything – whisky, gin, wine? I've got some beer in the fridge.

ALEC. Well, that would be fabulous, but we'll maybe try and get these done first? Before we lose the light.

ELIZABETH. Lose the light?

ALEC. Move that hand forward a bit – no, like this. (*Adjusts* ELIZABETH*'s hand.*) Right, let's try one now, shall we? Okay, chin down, eyes up, relax. Lovely.

Flash.

AGNES. Lose the light? A foundling. I am not found. I am lost. I appear to be rotting. Deconstructing, unravelling. I am living in reduced circumstances. As you might say. I have been . . . displenished.

Retriever. Imagine what this was like before it was converted. I am sure . . . no, I am sure of nothing. Perhaps I have bathed in the waters of Lethe. Crossed the river of forgetfulness. Perhaps I have forgot everything to do with my life here on this earth. Earth – circumference of: five hundred and eighty three million and four hundred thousand miles, atmosphere: mostly nitrogen and oxygen. Three-quarters of the Earth is covered by oceans. A little ball of blue and green spinning like a top through the inky iciness of space. The world and all its wonders. Office World. It is so cold here. There's such a draught. You're going to have to fit double glazing.

What do I know? Anything? Nothing? Something? The French Revolution – in May 1798 a meeting of the States General was called by Louis XVI. In June the Third Estate declared themselves a national assembly. In July the citizens – *citoyens* – of Paris rose up and stormed the Bastille. That will not get me far. The French are an immoral race, they keep mistresses.

Kiss of life, kiss of death. Life will find a way. Death also. I am dead. I do realise that. As in life so in death. Amo, amas, amat. Latin shmatin. Amo amas amat, I wish I had a cat. No that can't be right. But Latin is a dead language and I am dead so perhaps it is my native tongue.

Kings of Scotland – Robert the Bruce, David the Second, Robert the Second, Robert the Third, James the First, James the Second, James the Third . . . and so on . . .

Retriever. Reputation. Recant. Sleet. I feel sick.

I used to be – oh God, what did I used to be . . . before I was what I am now. Which is dead. I am all in darkness.

Wait – I remember! I am Agnes Soutar, spinster of this parish. The year is eighteen hundred and sixty-five. I am twenty-four-years old. I am a governess. I am found. I have risen up from the dust of the dead. I speak with my own tongue. I bring you, ladies and gentlemen, the past, sour and reeking, what was and what might have been.

Flash followed by darkness. Second flash, AGNES *sitting stiffly on sofa,* MERRIC *behind the camera.*

MERRIC. Excellent, Miss Soutar. Do you know, it's a curious thing but I am beginning to feel that nothing is exactly real until I have photographed it. I think that must be the mark of a true photographer. And is this not the Art of Truth? Shall we try one more? Very still now. Try not to breathe so much. Try not to look so distracted. (*Flash.*) There, now we have captured you for posterity.

AGNES. Like a butterfly.

MERRIC. A butterfly? How so?

AGNES. One captures a butterfly and sticks it on a pin.

MERRIC. One?

AGNES. A lepidopterist. You.

MERRIC. I am a mere amateur. An enthusiast. And besides, how else can we categorise? Form methodologies? Create classifications and taxonomies?

AGNES. Anthropologists do not stick people on pins. Are they not scientists?

MERRIC. One might claim they are not.

AGNES. Yes, but surely –

MERRIC. You are a most argumentative person.

AGNES. Forgive me.

MERRIC. Not at all. I find it rather charming in a member of the fairer sex. It is a shame God made lawyers to be men. And what do you know of anthropologists, Miss Soutar?

AGNES. My father was one, sir.

MERRIC. Really?

AGNES. Really. My mother died when I was a child. I accompanied my father on his travels around the world. I have seen much.

MERRIC. You are most surprising.

GERTIE *enters carrying a tray of tea.*

MERRIC. Ah, Gertie, the very person. Come, sit, you shall have your photograph taken.

GERTIE. Me?

MERRIC. Yes, you, Gertie.

AGNES. He is collecting women.

GERTIE. What?

MERRIC. Do not be alarmed, Miss Soutar jests.

AGNES. Do I?

GERTIE. What of the mistress's tea?

MERRIC. Sit, sit, there next to Miss Soutar. I am making portraits of all my servants.

AGNES (*to* MERRIC). A governess is not a servant.

MERRIC. No? What is she then? We are harbouring a socialist, Gertie! Be more cheerful, Gertie. Less terrified. You do not fear, as some primitive tribes are wont to, that the camera will steal your soul?

GERTIE (*alarmed*). Steal my soul?

AGNES. Only the devil can steal one's soul.

Enter LAVENDER.

LAVENDER. Here is my dearest, boy. And the new governess too.

MERRIC. Her name is Miss Soutar, Mother.

LAVENDER. It is hardly worth remembering their names, they come and go so fast. (*To* AGNES.) My son's wife is a virago, my dear. But what can you expect, her money came from trade. She will soon be rid of you. And anyway you are far too pretty. She will not tolerate that.

MERRIC. Now, now, Mother.

LAVENDER. Oh yes, one must watch one's tongue. Or the cat may get it. If only you had married for love. One should always marry for love, do you not agree, my dear?

AGNES. Well, yes.

LAVENDER. I married for love. A great love. My husband was a man of passion.

MERRIC. This is unseemly talk, Mother.

LAVENDER. Passion is not unseemly, it is as necessary to life as the beating of the heart. He was a sea captain, you know.

Captain Samuel Merric Chalmers. A hero. In the wars with
the Frenchman –

AGNES. Napoleon?

LAVENDER. A devilish froggy cur. My husband commanded
a frigate. He was so handsome in his uniform. My family
forbade me to see him. We met in secret, it was quite
thrilling. He has been dead these thirty years but there isn't
a day goes by when I do not miss him so.

MERRIC. Do not upset yourself, Mother.

LAVENDER. Yet I see him in my boy, he has his father's
features, but not his disposition. Captain Chalmers was very
carefree.

MERRIC. Careless, perhaps.

LAVENDER. His ship went down off the coast of Venezuela.
He said it was the voyage that was going to make his fortune.
He was always a romantic. He had gone to look for gold.

MERRIC. And found none.

LAETITIA *enters.*

LAETITIA. What is going on here? It is like a circus. Why not
bring in the bareback riders and the talking dogs.

LAVENDER. Talking dogs? Dogs have learnt to talk?

LAETITIA. Does no one in this house understand what a
drawing-room is for?

LAVENDER. Drawing?

LAETITIA. You are forever under my feet. Can you not go
somewhere and . . . darn something?

LAVENDER. Darn something? (*Exit* LAVENDER.)

MERRIC. I am taking portraits of the servants, my dear.

LAETITIA. In the drawing-room? You are a reputable lawyer
not a fairground photographer. Your amateur pursuits will be
the death of me. Is this my tea? It is cold. (*To* GERTIE.)
Fetch more, and take that dozy look off your face.

Exit GERTIE.

LAETITIA (*to* AGNES). Where are my children? Are they being left to their own devices again? The job of a governess is to . . .

MERRIC. Govern?

LAETITIA. Your levity is out of place, sir.

MERRIC. Perhaps Miss Soutar can report to me from the schoolroom? Are my daughters excelling in their geography and French – Bonjour, mademoiselle, comment allez-vous? Are Edith and Maude going to be exemplary Scotswomen?

LAETITIA. Perhaps Miss Soutar will explain the bad behaviour of the school room in her report.

AGNES. Bad behaviour?

LAETITIA. Noise. Shouting. *Laughter.*

MERRIC. Laughter? We certainly cannot have that.

LAETITIA. *Hysterical* laughter.

AGNES. I cannot recollect . . .

LAETITIA. Tuesday morning, twenty-two minutes past eleven.

MERRIC. Twenty-*two* minutes past eleven?

LAETITIA. Well?

AGNES. Twenty-two minutes past eleven on –

LAETITIA. Tuesday morning.

AGNES. Let me think. History, we were doing history. The French Revolution.

LAETITIA. And that is a humorous subject?

AGNES. Well, not in itself.

LAETITIA. Then what provided the source of such hilarity?

AGNES. I think it must have been when Edith was guillotining us. I was King Louis XVI and Maude was Queen Marie

Antoinette. Pretending to guillotine us I should say, of course. (*Pause.*) It was amusing at the time.

LAETITIA. I expect you would have had to have been there. What is that? A pluperfect subjunctive? Is that possible? You should know. Anyway – a little less history, I think – it is hardly going to be of any use to them in the future. The French are an immoral race. They keep mistresses. Have I made myself clear to you?

AGNES. Very clear.

LAETITIA. You are very . . . exotic-looking, Miss Soutar. Do you have foreign blood?

AGNES. My mother was Portuguese.

LAETITIA. And she is dead, is she not? And your father also? You have taken this position because you have found yourself in severely reduced circumstances. How would you manage in the world without employment? Without references? Without a reputation?

AGNES. I would not.

LAETITIA. A woman is nothing without a reputation. Nothing. Perhaps you should take care to remember that. You do not look like a governess, Miss Soutar, I trust you know how to behave like one.

AGNES. How should a governess look?

LAETITIA. Invisible, Miss Soutar, invisible.

Enter GERTIE *followed by* REV. SCOBIE.

GERTIE. A visitor for you, ma'am.

REV. SCOBIE. Mrs Chalmers.

MERRIC. I fear we have not been introduced, sir.

REV. SCOBIE. Reverend Charles Scobie, at your service, sir.

MERRIC. You are not the minister of our church.

REV. SCOBIE. No, I am the minister of my church, sir.

LAETITIA. Reverend Scobie and I have some business to discuss. It is of a private nature.

MERRIC. There are things to be kept private from me beneath my own roof?

LAETITIA. Things with which you need not be troubled. Are you not due in court?

MERRIC. You will allow me to finish Miss Soutar's portrait, I hope.

LAETITIA. I would rather you did not.

MERRIC. But I shall nevertheless, my dear.

LAETITIA. Then we shall await your absence in the parlour. Come Reverend Scobie.

LAETITIA, REV. SCOBIE *and* GERTIE *exit.* MERRIC *motions to* AGNES *to sit.*

AGNES. Have you not captured me yet, sir?

MERRIC. Are you making fun of me, Miss Soutar?

AGNES. I am not in a position to do that, sir. I am invisible.

MERRIC. Not to me you are not, Miss Soutar.

Flash.

ALEC. I think we're finished. (*Starts packing away his cameras etc.*)

ELIZABETH. It gets dark so early at this time of year. It's started to rain again. So, do you want a coffee now?

ALEC. No thanks.

ELIZABETH. Oh. Okay.

ALEC. I'd rather have a whisky.

ALEC *takes a step towards* ELIZABETH, *brushes a strand of hair out of her eyes.*

ALEC. I saw you once.

ELIZABETH. You saw me?

ALEC. Yes, I saw you once before. In the street. I thought you were the most beautiful woman I'd ever seen.

ELIZABETH. I can hardly believe that.

ALEC. No, you should. You should.

ALEC *kisses* ELIZABETH. *Lights fade slowly.*

AGNES. You will lose the light. You will lose everything.

ACT TWO

Scene 1

Four weeks later.

ALEC. Well, so . . . (*Kisses her.*) . . . Can I see you tonight?

ELIZABETH. You want to, do you?

ALEC. Yes . . . Absolutely. (*Kisses her.*) Yes. I want to see you every night. And anyway, it's our anniversary.

ELIZABETH. Our anniversary? Anniversary of what?

ALEC. Our first . . . meeting. A month together.

ELIZABETH. You old romantic you.

ALEC. Isn't that what women like? It's funny, isn't it?

ELIZABETH. What is?

ALEC. I don't know, fate, karma – whatever. I only came that day to take photographs. I never expected to end up in the sack with you. I might have been busy, when Kitty asked me. But I wasn't. And I am very glad. Very, very glad because I am crazy about you. Did I tell you I loved you?

ELIZABETH. About a hundred times last night.

ALEC. Ah, but that was in extremis, in the throes of passion, now I'm telling you in the cold and sober light of day.

ELIZABETH. You don't think, maybe we're going a bit fast with all this?

ALEC. Don't you trust your feelings? I know you're in love with me. And you're special, Elizabeth.

ELIZABETH. Special?

ALEC. Different. Not like the other women I've known. You're very, how can I put it . . . clear. Pure and clear. Strong,

I imagine you, I don't know, as . . . a medieval nun or a Victorian governess. Someone with standards and purpose.

ELIZABETH. A medieval nun? Are you joking? That sounds awful. I'd rather you saw me as someone with a gypsy soul, someone burning with flames of passion.

ALEC. But that's not you. You're Joan of Arc. Is that better – pure and strong, but with flames as well?

ELIZABETH. Maybe I'd rather you just saw me as me.

ALEC. I should get going. I should have been somewhere two hours ago.

ELIZABETH. What will you say?

ALEC. Oh, the usual excuse, three-car pile-up on the M8. Oh, yeah, by the way, what do you want to do for your birthday? Think about Paris for the weekend.

ELIZABETH. Really?

ALEC. Why not?

Kisses her. Enter CALLUM *from kitchen.*

CALLUM. Whoops, sorry.

ALEC. Hello . . . Callum.

CALLUM. Hello, Alec.

ALEC. Well, must go. See you tonight Lizzie. See you Callum.

CALLUM. Yeah.

Exit CALLUM *to bedroom. Enter* KITTY.

KITTY. Alec.

ALEC. Kitty.

Exit ALEC.

KITTY. You're still screwing the photographer, I see. You should be careful he's got a reputation. I mean I hope it's just a fling, I hope it's just sex.

ELIZABETH. Well, thanks for the sisterly advice but I'm all grown up and can look after myself.

KITTY. Oh God, that means you're taking it seriously.

ELIZABETH. Are you here for a reason or have you just come to annoy me?

KITTY. I've just come to annoy you. Are you going to give me a coffee?

ELIZABETH. Get it yourself, I'm going out.

KITTY. I've finished writing the article. Your article, about you. I brought it for you to read. I'll change anything you want. Just say.

ELIZABETH. I haven't got time now, just leave it on the table. Are you staying?

KITTY. I wanted Callum's advice. I'm thinking of buying a flat.

ELIZABETH. You're up to something.

KITTY. Me?

ELIZABETH. Hmm.

Exit ELIZABETH.

KITTY (*to* CALLUM). Would you like a coffee?

CALLUM. Cool. Thanks.

KITTY. Do you take sugar?

CALLUM. Three please.

KITTY. Three?

Enter CALLUM.

CALLUM. I'm a builder, I have to, *de rigueur*. As they say.

KITTY. Did you have a good weekend?

CALLUM. Me?

KITTY. Yes, you. I'm making polite conversation.

CALLUM. Yeah, top. Top weekend. Went to a sweat lodge.

KITTY. A sweat lodge? What an attractive idea.

CALLUM. In the Borders. It was amazing, totally fucking
    amazing. I had like this vision – (CALLUM's *mobile rings.*)
    Yeah, hi. No, I'm at work. Yeah, I know. No, I'll pick him
    up. I'll get something for tea, what do you fancy? I could do
    my bean stew thing. Sorted. Take care, bye.

KITTY. Your girlfriend?

CALLUM. Laura. She's great. Really together.

KITTY. Such a new man. So responsible.

CALLUM. Have I shown you a photograph of Finn?

KITTY. Finn?

CALLUM. My kid.

KITTY. Every time you say his name I think of our dog. It's
    very disturbing.

CALLUM. Sorry. (*Shows her the photograph.*)

KITTY. They all look alike to me really. (*Pause.*) So, my
    sister's in love.

CALLUM. Is she?

KITTY. Too busy to read the article I wrote. And re-wrote and
    re-wrote. I really wanted her to like it. And it's to help her,
    not me. I'm sure she doesn't believe me.

CALLUM. I'll read it.

KITTY. I want to do a good deed.

CALLUM. A good deed in a naughty world.

KITTY. Everyone seems to think I'm a bad person, but what
    have I done that's so bad, exactly?

CALLUM. I don't know.

KITTY. Ever since I can remember I've been treated as if I'd
    done something wrong. Elizabeth was 'mummy's little
    helper' but I was . . . and as for Daddy . . .

CALLUM. You weren't his little princess then? If I had a
    daughter she would be. I'd really like a girl next time. Laura

doesn't want another one yet. (*Pause.*) I'm sure they loved you really.

KITTY. Oh, don't speak platitudes Callum. The thing is, I don't think they actually loved either of us. Because I don't think either of them were capable of love. Not really.

CALLUM. I liked your mum.

KITTY. And I just feel . . . I just feel like something really bad happened to me. A really bad thing.

CALLUM. Well, maybe a really bad thing did happen to you and you can't remember.

KITTY. Oh that's too fucking easy, isn't it? Abuse, traumas, something nasty in the woodshed, untold horrors that you've suppressed. I'm not that lucky.

CALLUM. Lucky?

KITTY. No, it's much worse, because . . . I feel like a really bad thing happened to me. And it didn't. (*Starts to cry.*)

CALLUM. Someone needs a hug.

Puts his arms around her, they kiss.

Darkness.

Scene 2

AGNES *playing the piano. Enter* GERTIE.

GERTIE (*to* AGNES). Have you seen her anywhere?.

AGNES. Who?

GERTIE. The mistress. You shouldn't be in here.

AGNES. I have Mr Chalmers' permission to play the piano in here.

GERTIE. That will lead to an argument, for sure.

AGNES. People hate their governesses in the drawing-room. It reminds them that we are very little different from them.

GERTIE. When Adam delved and Eve span, who was then the gentleman?

AGNES. Seditious talk, Gertie. The master, for all his advanced ideas, still thinks we are born to a rank in this life from which we cannot depart.

GERTIE. Aye, we will never lord it over him.

AGNES. And yet we can move down the way. We can be cast out. As if from Paradise. I have lost everything.

GERTIE. I never had anything to lose.

AGNES. Oh Gertie, I have seen the world. I have seen the sun rise over the Matto Grosso. I have seen the whales swim around Cape Horn. This is a very narrow life we are leading, Gertie. It is as if we are shut in some small dark place from which we cannot see the sun and Mother Nature sporting all her fine bright colours – her gorgeous raiment and her cloudy bonnets with their rainbow ribbons.

GERTIE. Mother Nature?

AGNES. Do you not sometimes feel that your heart will burst from all the thoughts and emotions it is freighted with?

GERTIE. No.

AGNES. No, Gertie? Do you not sense the vibrations on the very air, like invisible messages from somewhere else, telling us how grand the world is, how fantastic our souls?

GERTIE. Only after a drop of gin.

AGNES. What will become of us, I wonder?

GERTIE. Become of us? When?

AGNES. When we die, when we are forgotten on this earth.

GERTIE. We pass over to the next life.

AGNES. What if there was nothing, if there was no next life? No God to raise us up?

GERTIE. Nothing?

AGNES. Nothing at all. Not us experiencing nothing, which is different, but nothing, a complete cessation of everything.

GERTIE. Too deep for me. And it is not what the Bible says.

AGNES. And what if the Bible were nothing but a pack of lies.

GERTIE (*puts her hands over her ears*). Amo, amas, amat, I wish I was a cat. You're mad. You're speaking black blasphemy.

AGNES. But imagine, Gertie – for just one minute – that these things were true, then how would we view our lives? Would we not snatch at whatever pleasure we could, would we not delight more in every dawn and sense the poignancy of every sunset? Would we not feel how delicious our lover's limbs felt entwined with ours, how sweet his breath, how precious every second on this earth must be.

GERTIE. He has had you too? He is a goat.

AGNES. A goat? Who?

GERTIE. He has had everything in a petticoat that has passed over this threshold.

AGNES. No indeed, no man has had me. That does not mean that I cannot see that love must be sublime. To have a grand passion. To feel the heart of another beating in rhythm with one's own?

GERTIE. You sound like the old woman. The mistress would not care if he had had you, not so long as she has her house. Look at her fine Brussels carpet and her overmantel cover that she embroidered herself in Turkey wools.

AGNES. Her antimacassars. Her overstuffed sofas like . . .

GERTIE. Hippopotamuses.

AGNES. Hippopotami. It is a Latin plural.

GERTIE. Latin shmatin. As if I care.

AGNES. Latin shmatin? Nonsense will get you nowhere. You should care. It is only through education that you will become their equal.

GERTIE. It hasn't worked for you.

AGNES. I seem to be having an unnecessarily unfortunate life.

MERRIC *enters, followed by* LAVENDER.

MERRIC. See what a magnificent example of a trilobite,
I found it at Ely. What do you think?

GERTIE. It's a lump of rock.

MERRIC. It is history, Gertie, living history, look, look closely.

GERTIE. It still looks like a lump of rock.

LAVENDER (*to* AGNES). My son is such an enthusiast. He is
very like his father in that respect. Captain Samuel
Chalmers, a great naval captain, commanded a frigate in the
wars against that French dog.

MERRIC. This little creature lived aeons ago, Gertie. This is
its imprint left behind. These 'lumps of rock' were sea-
dwelling animals that lived long before man and his
ancestors ever trod this earth.

GERTIE. You mean Adam and Eve?

MERRIC. I most certainly do not. Adam and Eve are creatures
of myth, akin to the great god Jupiter or the kelpie in the
burn. 'God' did not make us at all. Look at the world,
Gertie, in its vastness and its splendid arrangements.
Everything in its place, a place for everything, there is a
hierarchy and an order that is breathtaking, this is what
science shows us, Gertie. Science will drive out superstition
forever. Science has killed God.

AGNES. And that is a good thing?

MERRIC. Science is pure order!

LAVENDER. Killed God. Can God be killed?

MERRIC. There is no God, Mother. I believe in the glorious
order of creation, but not in a creator, no truly rational man
can believe such a thing.

AGNES. Nor a woman?

MERRIC. A rational woman? One may as well say a cold fire,
a green sun, a –

LAVENDER. Blue moon.

AGNES. No, they exist, for it is in that time that men perceive the intelligence of women.

GERTIE. In a blue moon?

AGNES. Once.

MERRIC. Miss Soutar is a wit, Mother. What say you, Miss Soutar, did God create the world in six days and then take tea on the seventh?

AGNES. Mr Chalmers is an evolutionist, Gertie, one of those who believes we are descended from monkeys.

MERRIC. The evolutionist does not believe in the fixity of species, he believes that the creatures of the natural world have adapted to their circumstances. For example, God did not 'create' the giraffe with a long neck, that is a variation which was useful to an animal feeding off tall trees –

AGNES. Natural selection.

MERRIC. You have read Mr Darwin, Miss Soutar?

LAVENDER. Monkeys? God made us from monkeys?

MERRIC. No, Mother. He did not.

AGNES. So you do not, like Mr Disraeli, wish to place yourself on the side of the angels?

MERRIC. No, Miss Soutar, I am on the side of the apes.

LAVENDER. Your father brought me a monkey back from his travels once. It was a dear little thing. My husband travelled the world, he brought back many curious things. I went with him aboard ship often before I had my dear son. What times we had.

MERRIC. And he left you with nothing.

LAVENDER. He left us with love.

MERRIC. He left us to live off handouts from the more charitable of your rich relations.

LAVENDER (*to* AGNES). I was disowned by my family when I married my darling husband. We eloped.

AGNES. Eloped?

LAVENDER. It was the most romantic adventure imaginable.

MERRIC. Or the most reckless folly.

AGNES. But you cannot chide your mother for her behaviour,
for if she had not eloped and married your father, you
would not exist.

MERRIC. Well, perhaps a better version of me would exist,
Miss Soutar.

AGNES. Better, how so? Is this one not good enough?

LAVENDER. I have not thought of that monkey in years.
It was such a dear little thing. It would sit at table with us
and eat so daintily. It died of a fever. I was quite heart-
broken. I had not realised how small it was until it died.

Enter LAETITIA.

It made such a little corpse.

LAETITIA. Leaving? Are you?

LAVENDER. Are we?

LAETITIA. Yes. I am at home to a visitor.

They exit. LAETITIA *sits on the sofa, holding mementoes of
her son.*

LAETITIA.
In the bright eternal city
Death can never never come
In His own good time He'll call us
From our rest to Home, Sweet Home.

REVEREND CHARLES SCOBIE *knocks on the door.*

REV. SCOBIE. Mrs Chalmers?

LAETITIA. Reverend Scobie, please come in.

REV. SCOBIE *enters.*

REV. SCOBIE. I rang the bell?

LAETITIA. Yes, I heard it.

REV. SCOBIE. But no one answered.

LAETITIA. Gertie is worse than useless. When God created servants I am sure he did not have Gertie in mind. I can hardly be expected to answer my own front door.

REV. SCOBIE. No, no, of course not.

LAETITIA. Shall we sit down? I'm afraid there is no tea. (*Rings the bell.*)

REV. SCOBIE. Because there is no Gertie?

LAETITIA. Exactly. I have a photograph of my boy. I thought it might perhaps help us, if we are to reach out to the other side?

REV. SCOBIE. That will not be necessary. The world of Spirit does not recognise objects on the material plane. To them such things are but shadows of the world they have left behind.

LAETITIA. And do they not miss this world, do they not cry out for us? George was but three years old. A baby. He was afraid of the dark. Even now I hear him calling to me in the night and I cannot comfort him.

REV. SCOBIE. My dear lady, do not upset yourself. He has a new home in Eternity. He is in the world of Spirit, he is not afraid. There is no fear on the other side.

LAETITIA. If I could just see his face one more time. He was snatched from my arms so suddenly. One day he was running around, playing with his dog out on the lawn, the next day struck down with a fever and gone. I had the dog killed. I could not bear to see it living while my poor little George lay cold in his coffin. They put my boy in the earth, in the dark, all alone. He must be so afraid.

REV. SCOBIE. My dear lady –

LAETITIA. I thought I could not bear it, I thought I could not live, but here I am, condemned to continue on this earth without my son.

REV. SCOBIE. The dead are all around us. As in life, so in death.

LAETITIA. What does that mean? What does that mean?

REV. SCOBIE. Let us seek comfort for you, Mrs Chalmers, let us make ourselves available to the Christian souls who wish to come over from the other side.

Dear God, we are sinners on this earth, lost and seeking, but if we believe we shall be found by the Shepherd and saved. Then we shall live in the world of Spirit and one day, at the very end of time we shall be resurrected.

Enter GERTIE, flustered.

GERTIE. Sorry, ma'am. I didn't hear the bell.

LAETITIA. How do you know it rang if you didn't hear it?

GERTIE. I don't know, ma'am.

LAETITIA. Your blouse is unfastened. Where is my husband?

GERTIE. In his study, I think, ma'am.

LAETITIA. You think? And yet you smell of his study. You reek of cheroots.

GERTIE. Shall I fetch the tea now, ma'am?

REV. SCOBIE. Sit, girl, you may help us reach out.

GERTIE. Where to?

REV. SCOBIE. To the dead.

GERTIE. I'd rather not, sir.

LAETITIA. Sit.

Lights go down.

REV. SCOBIE. Spirit beings, we are here to be a channel for your words, a conduit for your messages –

GERTIE *laughs.*

REV. SCOBIE. What is it, girl?

GERTIE. Messages.

REV. SCOBIE. Messages?

GERTIE. Shopping.

REV. SCOBIE. This is an uncalled for levity. You must comport yourself in a sober fashion, we are before God.

LAETITIA. Truly? You truly believe that?

REV. SCOBIE. Yes I do. Now let us commune with the Spirits. We must form a bridge between this world and the world of Spirit –

The lights go on suddenly. GERTIE *screams.* MERRIC *enters.*

MERRIC (*to* LAETITIA). You are at home to the charlatan, I see.

REV. SCOBIE. Charlatan?

MERRIC. You are not a true minister of the church. You are a purveyor of superstitious babble. You are an embarrassment to my house. Spiritualism! Hocus pocus, it is nearer to devil worship than Christianity. There are no such things as spirits. Come Gertie, my wife may suffer this unholy fool but I will not allow my servants to be corrupted by him.

Exit GERTIE.

LAETITIA. How dare you come bursting in here like some madman. Disturbing the peace of my house.

MERRIC. Your house?

LAETITIA. Yes, my house, sir. Bought with my money, on which you live like a parasite. The money which feeds your ridiculous pastimes and pursuits, which allows you to dabble in so-called science. Science cannot bring my boy back, can it?

MERRIC. Our boy. And you think this conjuror can bring him back? He has been dead these two years. George is gone, he is never coming back, he is rotting into the earth as we speak. He cannot be resurrected.

REV. SCOBIE. I will pray for you.

MERRIC. Pray do not trouble yourself, sir.

LAETITIA. I wish you in hell.

Darkness.

Scene 3

Two days later.

SUSIE. Joan of Arc? Jings, crivens and help ma Boab. What did he mean you reminded him of Joan of Arc?

ELIZABETH. Pure and strong with flames.

SUSIE. Flames?

ELIZABETH. Words aren't really his thing. He has more of a visual sense.

SUSIE. So it is serious then?

ELIZABETH. I think so. It feels serious. It feels . . . real. I don't know, it feels like I've come home, that here's someone who knows me.

SUSIE. I know you.

ELIZABETH. It's like we're . . . connected, at some deep level, it's almost spiritual.

SUSIE. You sound like Callum.

ELIZABETH. It's just I'm . . . happy.

SUSIE. Happy?

ELIZABETH. I can't think of another word for it. I feel . . . porous.

SUSIE. Porous? Happiness makes you feel porous? Like a colander? Am I ever going to meet him?

ELIZABETH. He's coming round later.

SUSIE. I was beginning to think he was a figment of your imagination.

ELIZABETH. And the nice thing is that he's so keen. None of that male holding back. He's fallen in love with me and he . . . admits it. So, I don't feel I have to hold back, you know. And all the barriers seem to have gone, between me and the world. Everything makes sense.

SUSIE. Are you going to eat those anchovies? Because I'll have them if you don't want them.

ELIZABETH. I feel like I'm not in control anymore and it's suddenly such a relief and at the same time it's still the scariest thing ever. But now I'm *in* the world. It's almost, I don't know . . . euphoric, Dionysian.

SUSIE. That's just good sex.

ELIZABETH. Maybe.

SUSIE. Kitty'll be annoyed if she thinks you're happy.

ELIZABETH. She's jealous.

SUSIE. Tell me something new.

ELIZABETH. She's full of doom and gloom, says he has a terrible reputation, that I'm going to get hurt.

SUSIE. So does he photograph you?

ELIZABETH. Photograph me?

SUSIE. Yeah, he's a photographer, does he take photographs?

ELIZABETH. All the time, he says he can't see a thing properly until he's photographed it.

SUSIE. That's very profound. I thought he was just a staff photographer on Kitty's rag.

ELIZABETH. Well, yeah but that's just to earn money, I mean he's got serious stuff he does for himself, arty stuff, you know, like for exhibitions. They're really good, moody black and white pictures of trees and water. Very Romantic. With a capital R. He's romantic with a small r, do you know what, he said that –

SUSIE. And how are you, Susie? How's your life going – conceived a baby yet?

ELIZABETH. I'm sorry. (*Pause.*) So how *are* you?

SUSIE. So-so. Not in a state of Dionysian abandonment, that's for sure.

ELIZABETH. No? And Jo?

SUSIE. I don't know. We haven't been getting on very well. We had a really bad fight last night. I don't even know what it was about. Something's changed between us. I looked at her and I thought, 'I don't really know you anymore'. Sometimes I wonder if we aren't having a baby just to keep us together.

ELIZABETH. Just like . . .

SUSIE. Just like what?

ELIZABETH. Nothing.

SUSIE. No, no, you were going to say something.

ELIZABETH. No I wasn't.

SUSIE. You were going to say 'Just like normal couples'.

ELIZABETH. No, I wasn't.

SUSIE. Don't lie to me.

ELIZABETH. Susie . . .

SUSIE. Susie what?

ELIZABETH. I didn't mean it like that.

SUSIE. You think, deep down, that my life isn't as valid as yours, don't you?

ELIZABETH. Valid?

SUSIE. You're still playing fucking Queen for a Day, aren't you? And oh, being gay's all very well, and it's quite interesting that your best friend's gay but when push comes to shove, my relationship isn't as important as yours somehow.

ELIZABETH. Now you are being ridiculous.

SUSIE. Am I?

ELIZABETH. Why are we fighting?

SUSIE. I don't know. I'm sorry. I'm not in a good mood. I have this feeling that things are falling apart, as if I'm not in control any more. I don't understand what's happening.

ELIZABETH. I've never understood what was happening.

SUSIE. I got my period –

ELIZABETH. Oh, that'll be it then, that's why you're cranky, it's just PMT.

SUSIE. No, I got my period.

ELIZABETH. Yes, I heard you.

SUSIE. As in 'I got my period therefore I'm not pregnant'.

ELIZABETH. Oh, right. Well, it's early days, isn't it?

The phone rings.

ELIZABETH. Hi. No, no, no I'm not doing anything. Susie's here. Just talking. Oh what a shame. It's okay. Of course I do. Okay. Bye then. (*Laughs.*) Bye. (*Pause.*) Bye. (*Laughs.*) I'm putting the phone down, okay? Now. Goodbye. (*To* SUSIE.) What?

SUSIE. Nothing.

ELIZABETH. He's not coming round. He got held up. A three-car pile-up on the M8.

Darkness.

Scene 4

MERRIC *sitting on the sofa, head in hands. Enter* AGNES.

AGNES. I am sorry, I did not mean to disturb you, I left my music in here.

MERRIC. Please – Miss Soutar, do not go.

AGNES. Are you not well, sir?

MERRIC. No I am not 'well' Miss Soutar. I am in a black pit of despair.

AGNES. I am sorry for you.

MERRIC. Do you ever feel, Miss Soutar, that you have wings on your back, great powerful wings that have never been

unfolded and shaken out to dry in the morning sun. That
you will never fly because of the . . . constraints upon you.

AGNES. Constraints?

MERRIC. Of society. Of expectations. Of the small domestic
life.

AGNES. Perhaps we are only as constrained as we allow
ourselves to be.

MERRIC. 'A man who dares to waste an hour of life has not
discovered the value of life'. Do you know who said that,
Miss Soutar?

AGNES. Mr Darwin.

MERRIC. Mr Darwin. He of the wide horizons and unbounded
life.

AGNES. Does a man not make his own destiny?

MERRIC. You know I married my wife for her fortune. I did
not marry for love. I do not think I have ever experienced
love. I yearn for a gentle touch, for a heart that understands.

AGNES. I am sorry for your pain.

MERRIC. You are very sorry today.

AGNES. But not for myself.

MERRIC. You still have your hopes, Miss Soutar.

AGNES. And so should you, sir.

MERRIC. Well, who is to say, Miss Soutar, perhaps I do,
perhaps I do.

AGNES. You have much. I have nothing. I am an orphan,
without relative or friend in this world. And yet I am
cheerful.

MERRIC. I shall be your friend. (*Takes her hand.*)

AGNES. Do not do this, sir.

MERRIC. Why not?

AGNES. Do not do this to me, sir.

MERRIC. Miss Soutar, I cannot remain dumb. My feelings for you can no longer be kept unspoken.

AGNES. And yet to voice them goes beyond the bounds of what is acceptable.

MERRIC. What is acceptable? I did not think you such a captive to social propriety.

AGNES. I have a reputation. The only thing I have is a reputation.

MERRIC. I dwell on you constantly. You haunt my waking hours. You walk through my dreams like an apparition. You are an infection in my brain, you flow through my veins like a sweet poison. It is a desire you feel also and you are a liar, Miss Soutar, if you deny it. And you are not a liar, Miss Soutar.

AGNES. Nor am I denying it. But I still ask you to desist, sir.

MERRIC. Let us be united in that final abandonment. Consumed in the flames of passion.

AGNES. I am fearful.

MERRIC. There is nothing to fear. I will let no harm befall you.

AGNES. I am fearful of the unknown. I am standing on the edge of a precipice and I do not know if I shall fall or fly.

MERRIC. Oh, you will fly, Miss Soutar, you will fly. Trust me. We have been led east of Eden, let us regain Paradise for ourselves. We will be a new Adam and Eve, holy innocents in our garden of heavenly delights.

AGNES. And yet look what happened to them when they succumbed to the forbidden fruit.

MERRIC. They gained knowledge, Miss Soutar – the most thrilling reward of all.

Enter LAETITIA. *They embrace. Darkness.*

Scene 5

Two weeks later.

MERRIC. Lying with you is like lying with an angel.

AGNES. I doubt angels do the things we do.

MERRIC. There would be little point in going to heaven then.

AGNES. I fear that is not our destination.

MERRIC. Truly at this moment I believe in the existence of cherubim and seraphim and all of the archangels. (*Kisses her.*) And they are all inhabiting this pretty corporeal host.

AGNES. What strange blasphemy a man can speak in extremis.

MERRIC. This argumentative corporeal host.

AGNES. Is it not extraordinary that every breath which rises in your chest seems of the utmost importance to me. You are like a planet newly-discovered and uncharted by any explorer. Every eyelash, each fingernail, the map of veins beneath the skin, the streams of blood which course throughout the whole.

MERRIC. You are most imaginative.

AGNES. It is love which has made me so. These past two weeks have rendered me . . . sensible.

MERRIC. Sensible?

AGNES. Sensible of the world around me. I feel as if I am living every moment as if it were my last, drinking in every sensation. I can hear the spiders walk across the cellar ceiling. I can see into the craters of the moon and hear the dormouse snore. I can hear the planets whispering to each other across the blackness of space. I am like a spirit that can fly across the oceans. I am porous to the wind. I am feverish with love.

ALEC. Christ, I've got another erection.

ELIZABETH. Do you look like your father?

ALEC. What?

ELIZABETH. Your father, does he look like you?

ALEC. I hope not, he's dead.

ELIZABETH. Does your brother look like you?

ALEC. My brother? No, not really. Your sister doesn't look like you.

ELIZABETH. She's not my sister.

ALEC. How can your sister not be your sister? Is this like one of those mind games?

ELIZABETH (*pause*). Because I was *adopted*.

ALEC. Oh yeah, of course, I forgot.

ELIZABETH. How could you forget?

ALEC. Sorry. Why are you so interested in my family?

ELIZABETH. Well . . . because that's where you come from. I'm interested in everything about you. I'd like to meet your family.

ALEC. Why?

ELIZABETH. I don't know. I'd like to know what they're like. Why is that so odd? I'm always curious about people's families, I suppose because I don't have one.

ALEC. What about your sister?

ELIZABETH. No, I mean, I don't know my background.

ALEC. You should live in the moment. I try to do that. It saves a lot of hassle, believe me.

AGNES. What about your wife?

MERRIC. My wife?

AGNES. She is not likely to die.

MERRIC. Everyone dies. It is our one certainty. We die and we are gone forever.

AGNES. I mean soon. She will not die soon. Unfortunately. She is young, well, youngish, as healthy as an ox. Am I doomed to be a mistress for the rest of my life, I ask myself?

MERRIC. The rest of your life? We may die tomorrow, we must live in the moment.

AGNES. I am not so lacking in virtue as you would seem to think. I wish to be a wife. I wish to keep my reputation. I would like children.

ELIZABETH. I wonder what our children would look like?

ALEC. Children? We've only known each other six weeks.

ELIZABETH. I wonder what Susie's baby will look like, if she ever manages to have one.

ALEC. Susie?

ELIZABETH. I mean it will look like her, but it won't look like her and Jo, it'll look like her and someone anonymous. Would you donate sperm to a sperm bank?

ALEC (*looks at his watch*). I should get going.

ELIZABETH. Aren't you going to stay?

ALEC. Can't. Sorry. Early start. Sorry. (*Kisses her.*) I'll give you a ring.

ELIZABETH. You haven't forgotten tomorrow?

ALEC. Tomorrow?

ELIZABETH. My birthday? My mother's coming round and Susie, my best friend who you haven't met yet, and my sister. Kitty. Remember? Kitty?

ALEC. Yeah, Kitty. Of course, I haven't forgotten. I'll be there. One o'clock. On the dot.

AGNES. When shall we meet?

MERRIC. We will find a moment. I must go. (*Exit* AGNES.)

Enter LAVENDER.

LAVENDER. You have weighed yourself down with an anchor. An anchor that goes by the name of Laetitia. You are drowning on account of it.

MERRIC. This is an old theme.

LAVENDER. But now there is a new variation on it.

MERRIC. How so?

LAVENDER. You are in love.

MERRIC. That is a nonsense.

LAVENDER. It is true, look at you, you have lightness in your step. You smile for no reason. You have felt fire in your belly. She has made you alive.

MERRIC. What would you have me do? Run off with her?

LAVENDER. Yes!

MERRIC. You are a fool, Mother.

LAVENDER. No, you are the fool. And you are a coward. Not like your father.

MERRIC. A coward?

LAVENDER. You're afraid because your wife will sue you for desertion if you leave. You will lose her money.

MERRIC. I will lose everything that gives a man his character.

LAVENDER. Your character has been forged by Mammon.

MERRIC. I will not stay to hear this talk.

Exit MERRIC.

LAVENDER. One should follow one's heart.

AGNES. Shall I light the lamps?

LAVENDER. Oh what a fright you gave me, I thought you were a ghost.

AGNES. Can you not sleep? Would you like me to read to you?

LAVENDER. Come and sit here by me and tell me the secrets of your heart.

AGNES. What if I have none?

LAVENDER. You do, I can see it in the blush on your cheek. You have felt the touch of passion's hand, you need not deny it to me, I am your friend in this house. Let me be your confidante. You are in love with my son.

AGNES. These things should not be talked about.

LAVENDER. You can talk about them to me. Tell me, tell me how you feel.

AGNES. I feel . . .

LAVENDER. Tell me.

AGNES. I feel as if I am floating above the earth, as if I know all of life's secrets. As if I have been blessed. As if I am in a state of grace. As if I could reach out and touch the future.

LAVENDER. That is love. That is what love does for you.

AGNES. But it is a love which is impossible.

LAVENDER. Why? My son loves you. For the first time in his life he has the chance to listen to his heart instead of the voice of reason. Reason – I do not give a fig for reason and neither should you.

AGNES. But there is no room in this world for such a love.

LAVENDER. Then you must make room.

Darkness.

Scene 6

The next day. SUSIE *and* ELIZABETH *setting the table,* CALLUM *working.*

CALLUM. I'm off then.

ELIZABETH. Not going to stay for lunch? And you had such a good time the last time. My mother was probably looking forward to discussing her operations with you and many more of our dark family secrets, our skeletons in the cupboard.

CALLUM. I think once was enough, thanks.

Exit ELIZABETH *to kitchen.*

SUSIE. Kitty will be disappointed.

CALLUM. Will she?

SUSIE. Are you all right? You seem very down today. Are you okay? Are you crying, Callum?

CALLUM. My girlfriend left me.

SUSIE. Laura?

CALLUM. She took Finn.

SUSIE. I thought you were so . . . sorted.

CALLUM. We were, then I fucked it all up. I fucked someone else. I can't believe I could be so fucking stupid.

SUSIE. I don't know what to say.

Enter ELIZABETH.

ELIZABETH. Oh dear.

SUSIE. Laura left him. Took Finn. Infidelity. His.

CALLUM. I don't know how it happened, one minute I was working, the next minute –

ELIZABETH. In my house?

CALLUM. She was upset.

SUSIE. Who? Who was upset?

CALLUM. Kitty.

ELIZABETH *and* SUSIE. Kitty?

ELIZABETH. You screwed Kitty, in my house? When? Where?

The doorbell rings. KITTY *lets herself and* INA *in.*

KITTY. Only us. Happy birthday. (*Kisses* ELIZABETH.)

INA. It's raining stair-rods out there. Where's the birthday girl? Happy birthday then. Hello, Susie.

SUSIE *kisses* INA *on the cheek.*

INA. How continental everyone is these days. Callum's got his feet under the table, I see.

CALLUM. I'm just going.

INA. Have you been crying? Has he been crying? I don't like to see a man cry.

KITTY (*to* CALLUM). Don't go on my account.

ELIZABETH. You're unbelievable, Kitty.

KITTY. Me? Why?

INA. What have you done to your hair?

Exit CALLUM.

SUSIE. If it moves, fuck it, eh, Kitty?

KITTY. It takes two for Christ's sake. I'm not a vampire.

INA. What are you two talking about?

KITTY. Have you done something to your hair?

INA. That's what I said. She looks different.

ELIZABETH. He's split up with his girlfriend.

INA. You shouldn't be cooking on your birthday. You never go out. You haven't got that disease have you?

ELIZABETH. I'm not cooking, it's all cold. Salad. Quiche.

KITTY. He's not a victim. We're grown up, we fucked, end of story.

INA. Quiche. We called it flan in my day. Cheese flan. You put such a lot of effort into things. Some might say too much but personally I don't think people put enough effort into things. Well, anyway, happy birthday. More or less.

KITTY. We might even have had some genuine feelings for each other.

INA. So, is Elizabeth's new man joining us then? Does he have a good job? Does he have a job?

ELIZABETH. He's a photographer.

INA. A photographer.

KITTY. Everything isn't always my fault.

INA. What on earth are you going on about? Me, me, me, Kitty, all the time, you should learn to take an interest in other people.

SUSIE. I think she should stop taking an interest in other people.

INA. So, Susie, how are you?

KITTY. Knocked up yet?

INA. I beg your pardon?

SUSIE. My partner – Jo – and I have been trying to start a family.

INA. There, you see, Susie's got normal instincts, and *she's* a scientist. And she's got a partner now. I didn't know that, Susie. How nice for you, dear. Wouldn't you like to get married, Susie? First? Before you have a baby. Does no one do that anymore? And what does Jo do, got a good job, has he?

SUSIE. Jo's a doctor. She works very hard.

Silence.

INA. A doctor? Very nice.

KITTY. You didn't know that, did you? Didn't know that Susie was gay. Perfect little Susie, always such a good girl, always well-behaved is a lesbian.

Pause.

INA. Well, she's still the same Susie, isn't she? (*To* ELIZABETH.) You're not a . . . one, are you? Maybe that's your problem.

ELIZABETH. Problem? I have a problem? What about Kitty? Maybe she's gay?

KITTY. Me?

SUSIE. I don't fancy her.

ELIZABETH (*to* INA). Maybe everyone's gay.

SUSIE. It's not the end of the world.

INA. Well, it would be if everyone was . . . like that.

KITTY. The end of the world.

ELIZABETH. No, I mean it's not like sleeping with your sister's husband, is it?

INA. I don't understand how a . . .

SUSIE. Lesbian.

INA. How a lesbian can have a baby.

KITTY. You go to a sperm bank.

INA. A sperm bank?

ELIZABETH. It's not like the Clydesdale.

INA. I should hope not. So then the baby will have . . . two mothers.

KITTY (*to* ELIZABETH). Just like you. Have you told her?

INA. Well, well. And who will . . . ?

SUSIE. I don't know. I don't know if we're going to go ahead just yet. We've hit a bit of a rough patch at the moment. Jo and I.

INA. Just like normal people.

KITTY (*to* ELIZABETH). You haven't told her have you?

INA. Told me what? Is someone dead?

KITTY. I don't believe you, Elizabeth.

ELIZABETH. There's going to be a piece in the paper tomorrow. Kitty wrote it.

KITTY. Thank you. About Elizabeth.

INA. I don't understand.

ELIZABETH. Kitty's written an article for her newspaper about how I was abandoned. As a baby.

KITTY. To try and find her mother.

INA. I'm her mother.

KITTY. You know what I mean.

INA. I don't. I don't know why you want to find *her*. I've been a good mother to you, haven't I?

Silence.

SUSIE. Of course you have.

ELIZABETH (*to* INA). It's got nothing to do with you. It's about me. I need to know what happened, how she feels, I'd like to know how she feels –

INA. She dumped you. It was as good as murder. It *was* murder.

ELIZABETH. It's to do with, I don't know – my sense of . . . self.

INA. Selfish, more like.

ELIZABETH. I just want to know. There's no reason for you to be upset.

INA. I'm the one who's brought you up, looked after you, paid for everything. *She* didn't want you. *She* left you to die.

ELIZABETH. And I want to know why.

INA. I did the best I could, but it was never enough for either of you was it? I'd like to see what kind of a job you'd make of being a mother, Elizabeth. You're so wrapped up in yourself it would probably never get its nappy changed. (*To* SUSIE.) When you look at how these two behave doesn't it make you think twice?

SUSIE. Think twice about what?

INA. Having one. A baby. Maybe you'd go about it a different way, being . . .

SUSIE. Gay.

INA. And it's quite . . . legal?

SUSIE. Yes.

INA. Well, I don't suppose it's so very odd. Every woman wants a baby. I think you'd make a good mother, Susie.

ELIZABETH (*to* INA). And it will know its real mother.

SUSIE. Oh God, here we go again.

ELIZABETH. What do you mean?

SUSIE. We were talking about me not you. 'Oh I was an abandoned baby, my mother didn't want me, they left me to die, who am I? Who am I really? How can I ever know?'

ELIZABETH. I don't behave like that.

SUSIE. Yes you do.

ELIZABETH (*to* SUSIE). How can you say that?

SUSIE. I always have be there for you. Who was it who picked up the pieces after Gregor? I'm beginning to see why he did it, at least Kitty doesn't moan all the time.

KITTY. Thanks.

ELIZABETH. What?

SUSIE. You're totally self-obsessed. I spent hour after hour, night after night listening to you after you left Gregor. And now you're so-called happy, you're even worse. 'Oh, he fucks like an angel, Susie', 'I don't think I've ever felt like this before.' You don't really want to hear the same from me do you? 'Jo fucks like an angel, Elizabeth' – in fact, you don't want to hear anything from me. Look actually I think I'm going to go. This is just getting . . . nasty.

Goodbye, Liz. I'll phone you later. (*Exits.*)

INA. Dear me, I hope your young man comes soon or we might have to start our lunch without him. He's very late, your young man.

KITTY. Alec.

ELIZABETH. Oh my God . . .

SUSIE. What? (*Pause*.) What?

ELIZABETH (*to* KITTY). You've slept with him, haven't you? You've slept with Alec. You've slept with every other man on the planet why would you have left him out?

KITTY. It was ages ago.

SUSIE. Ages? You've only been back up here a few months.

KITTY. It didn't mean anything, it was just sex.

ELIZABETH. It means something to me.

KITTY. Oh for God's sake, he's shagged just about everyone under fifty at the newspaper.

ELIZABETH. Before or after?

KITTY. Before or after what?

ELIZABETH. Me. Before or after me.

KITTY. Before, of course.

ELIZABETH. Liar.

KITTY. No.

INA. Is this Elizabeth's new boyfriend we're talking about?

Kitty hasn't . . . with him, has she? She doesn't get that kind of behaviour from me.

ELIZABETH. How long before?

KITTY. I don't know.

ELIZABETH. How long?

KITTY. The day he came to take the photographs. That was the last time. *Before* he took the photographs.

ELIZABETH. The same day? You are such a fucking whore.

KITTY. And he isn't?

INA. I don't know what the world's coming to. In my day you met someone, fell in love, married them and stayed with them until one of you died. I remember a time when you could be certain about things.

KITTY. But it was an illusion.

INA. I liked my illusions.

KITTY. When I tried to kill myself, was that an illusion?

INA. You did no such thing. It was an accident.

KITTY. Have you looked at me once and seen how unhappy I am. And wondered why?

INA. Why? Why are you so unhappy?

KITTY. I don't know. I feel like a very bad thing happened to me –

ELIZABETH. Oh you and your fucking bad thing, Kitty. A bad thing didn't happen to you, you do bad things. Sleeping with Alec, sleeping with Gregor –

KITTY. Don't forget Callum.

INA. Gregor? Your husband? What nonsense, tell her you did no such thing, Kitty. Kitty? You didn't, you didn't sleep with your sister's husband?

KITTY. Just keeping it in the family.

ELIZABETH. There's lots of things you don't know about Kitty.

INA. Such as?

KITTY. Shut up now, do you hear me.

ELIZABETH. Why?

INA. When Elizabeth was married to him? When you 'slept with' Gregor, was Elizabeth still married to him?

ELIZABETH. That was why she had the abortion. (*To* KITTY.) Wasn't it?

INA. Abortion? I don't understand.

ELIZABETH. She was having Gregor's baby.

KITTY. Well that was more than you managed.

ELIZABETH *slaps* KITTY. *Silence.*

INA. I don't know what's happened to you two. You didn't learn that kind of behaviour from me.

KITTY. No, we learned it from Dad. He hit you all the time.

INA. Not this nonsense again.

KITTY. How can you say it's nonsense? He was a violent bully. He despised you, he had no respect for you at all.

INA. Neither do you. And you don't know what you're talking about.

KITTY. We were there, we're witnesses. It was our history as well as yours and now you pretend it never happened.

INA. We were happy.

KITTY. No, we were not. How could any of us have been happy living with Dad? He's dead now, he can't do anything to you. He's not going to come back from the grave to give you a good sorting out. That was his phrase, wasn't it? A good sorting out. Do you remember that time Dad locked you in the coal-cellar?

INA. I don't know what you're talking about. He did no such thing.

KITTY. Of course he did. And the time he hit you so hard with the poker that you had to go to hospital. He broke every single piece of crockery in the kitchen because you hadn't cooked anything for his tea once. Every time he had a drink he hit you. (*To* ELIZABETH.) Are you just going to stand there or are you going to say something?

ELIZABETH (*to* INA). She's right, you know she's right. Dad was a vicious man.

Silence.

KITTY. He killed Finn, he killed our dog.

INA. That was an accident.

ELIZABETH. No it wasn't. You know it wasn't. You were there. The dog was trying to protect you.

KITTY. Dad was hitting you.

ELIZABETH. And Finn was barking at him, trying to stop him. And we were screaming and screaming at him not to do it.

KITTY. And he just kept kicking and kicking him until he was dead.

INA. Maybe you should be glad he killed the dratted dog and not me.

KITTY. We loved the dog.

INA. And you didn't love me, is that what you're saying? You have no idea, you have no idea about anything. All I ever hear from you both is 'me this', 'me that'. What about me? How do you think I feel about me? What do I think when I look back on forty years of marriage with Daddy? What kind of a waste has my life been? *You're* not happy? What about me? Not once in my life, not for one hour, not one minute, have I ever been happy. And nobody, not one person in the whole world cares. You think you're both so clever both of you, but you're not kind.

KITTY. Neither are you.

INA. Then you know where you got it from. And I've had enough of all this, I really have. I tell you what – fuck you.

Exit INA. *Silence.*

KITTY. Happy birthday.

Darkness.

Scene 7

A few days later. Darkness followed by a flash. ELIZABETH *is standing by the window.*

ELIZABETH. Don't.

ALEC. Why not.

ELIZABETH. I don't like it. You know I don't like being photographed.

ALEC. I'm sorry I missed your birthday.

ELIZABETH. I'm glad you did. We weren't at our best. As you might say. Where've you been, I've been trying to get hold of you.

ALEC. Sorry. I've had a lot of stuff on.

ELIZABETH. See the moon?

ALEC. Yeah.

ELIZABETH. And the stars?

ALEC. Yeah.

ELIZABETH. We could go out for a walk.

ALEC. Yeah, okay, if you want. It's cold out though.

ELIZABETH. What are you doing?

ALEC. What does it look like I'm doing? I'm re-loading the camera.

ELIZABETH. Are you going to take more photographs?

ALEC. No, I was going to paint a picture.

ELIZABETH. There's no need to be like that. Shall we go out for a walk then?

ALEC. I said yes.

ELIZABETH (*looking out of the window*). That's a really bright star, it must be Venus. The evening star. Of course, it's the morning star as well, isn't it? Is it? 'Oh she doth hang upon the cheek of night like a rich jewel in an Ethiop's ear'. Did I quote that correctly?

ALEC. What are you talking about?

ELIZABETH. Nothing. It's a new moon, we should wish on it.

ALEC. I could try and photograph it.

ELIZABETH. I don't want to photograph it, I want to remember it. You haven't even looked at it.

ALEC. Yes, I have. What are you getting so upset about?

ELIZABETH. You fucked my sister.

ALEC. Not recently.

ELIZABETH. Why didn't you tell me?

ALEC. Why should I? What's it got to do with you?

ELIZABETH. She's my *sister*.

ALEC. I thought she wasn't.

ELIZABETH. That's a technicality.

ALEC. If you're going to start sounding like a lawyer, I'm going.

ELIZABETH. Do you love me?

ALEC. I thought you wanted to go out.

ELIZABETH. I've changed my mind.

ALEC. Look. (*Pause.*) I've been thinking, Elizabeth, I think we should cool it a bit.

ELIZABETH. What do you mean, cool it?

ALEC. Just that. I think we should cool it for a bit. You're being very intense about all this.

ELIZABETH. Intense?

ALEC. Yes, intense. We hardly know each other and you've got us dead and buried in a joint plot with the grandchildren looking on.

ELIZABETH. So you think we should – what – see less of each other?

ALEC. Not see each other at all.

ELIZABETH. You said you loved me.

ALEC. I said I was crazy about you. I'm always crazy about women when I sleep with them and then . . . you're a great fuck –

ELIZABETH. Oh, thank you.

ALEC. I didn't mean to hurt you. Look, I like you, Elizabeth, I really do, but I just don't want to settle down for the rest of my life with you. Or with anyone, not right now. It was lust, for God's sake. I mean, what is it, you have sex with someone and then you're supposed to be together for the rest of your life? We're more adult than that, aren't we?

ELIZABETH. Are we?

ALEC. You're not really my type. You're too . . . nice.

ELIZABETH. *Nice*?

ALEC. I'm not *your* type. I don't want the things you want. It was great, but there's no future in it. I don't want you thinking there is. I'm sorry you fell for me so heavily, I really am, but I just don't feel the same way about you. I'm not the person you think I am. I haven't got any answers for you.

ELIZABETH. Answers? I don't even know the questions.

ALEC. We can still go out for a walk if you want.

ELIZABETH. Look, let's be mature about this, we can be sensible. It's illogical of me to be upset about Kitty, she didn't know we were going to . . . I can get over it. I love you, I want to make it work.

ALEC. Well, I don't Elizabeth. Okay? It's over for me, I'm not interested any more.

ELIZABETH. You're just saying that.

ALEC. Yeah, I am, I'm just saying it.

ELIZABETH. Please don't go. I don't think you realise what we have. You'll be sorry, you'll live to regret it. I know how you feel about me, you love me.

ALEC. Elizabeth, watch my lips, goodbye. Okay. Goodbye.

Exit ALEC. *The phone rings.*

ELIZABETH. Alec? Oh no, sorry. Hello. She what? Yes, yes, I will. Okay. Thanks. (*Puts the phone down. Silence. Picks it up and dials again.*) Kitty? Kitty, you won't believe this.

She's got in touch. She's got in touch with the paper. Who?
My mother. My real mother. She wants to meet me. Kitty,
I need you.

Darkness.

Scene 8

LAETITIA and REVEREND SCOBIE *sitting at the table.*

REV. SCOBIE. Spirit beings, we wish to make contact with
the other side. We pray humbly for your assistance –

LAETITIA. I am thinking of getting rid of the governess.

REV. SCOBIE. For what reason?

LAETITIA. Because I can. Because my husband is in love
with her.

REV. SCOBIE. Husbands can be very vexatious in my
experience. Your husband is a godless man. He will wander
in the spiritual wilderness, a soul lost forever in eternal
darkness.

LAETITIA. I am a wife who is neglected by her husband.
I believe I am a woman despised by her husband. I long for
a comforting hand.

REV. SCOBIE. You may have mine, dear lady. I am a man of
God.

LAETITIA. Don't be so ridiculous. The time has come to put
an end to this dalliance. You have failed me, Charles. You
promised me my son but you have shown me nothing but
tricks. I hate to say this, God knows I do, but my husband
was right, you are little short of a hoaxer.

REV. SCOBIE. No! You merely lack belief.

LAETITIA. Merely? I wish you to leave my house. Now. Be
gone, man. Now, this instant. Go.

Exit REVEREND SCOBIE.

LAETITIA. Dear Lord, forgive me, I have forgot my Christian duties as a wife. Cleanse this house of the sin and corruption which has infected it –

Enter MERRIC.

MERRIC. You have been entertaining your friend again, I see.

LAETITIA. He has gone. For good. We must put our house to rights. All is chaos and confusion within these walls. We are descending into a state of anarchy. We must pray for the return of good government. Do you understand? (*Pause.*) Do you understand?

MERRIC. I understand.

Exit MERRIC.

LAETITIA. Gertie!

Enter GERTIE.

GERTIE. Madam?

LAETITIA. The place is in complete disorder. We must do something about the state of this house. Do I make myself clear?

GERTIE. Yes, ma'am.

Exit LAETITIA. *Enter* AGNES.

AGNES. I am late.

GERTIE. It is nothing but lateness in this house. One big . . . lateness.

AGNES. I am late.

GERTIE. So you said.

AGNES. No, I mean I think I am with child.

GERTIE. Have you tried gin?

AGNES. Gin?

GERTIE. A knitting needle, a hot bath, jumping off a table, you have to get rid of it.

AGNES. Kill my child?

GERTIE. There's no good wringing your hands and moaning. That won't help you. There's no future for you if you don't.

AGNES. I know.

GERTIE. What will become of you?

AGNES. Oh, Gertie, I am fearful. Something is happening. It is beginning, Gertie.

GERTIE. Beginning? What is beginning?

AGNES. The end. I am afraid.

Exit GERTIE.

AGNES. Where are you going? Don't go. I am frightened of the dark.

Darkness.

Scene 9

A week later.

ELIZABETH. God. I need a drink.

KITTY. A big one. I'm amazed.

ELIZABETH. At what?

KITTY. That she actually responded to the article. It was such a slim chance. (*Pours a drink for both of them.*)

ELIZABETH. That was . . . She was . . . not what I was expecting really. But what was I expecting? Someone . . . mythic. A woman who'd had her baby wrenched from her against her will and spent the last forty years pacing this earth looking for her child –

KITTY. Not someone who got knocked up down at the swing park by a boy called Kenny. Well, at least we know you're not really a princess. 'Two sons. Doing very well. David's married to a lovely girl, Lesley. First baby on the way. Married to Bill for thirty years. Never told him about her "mistake". No point in rocking the boat now.'

ELIZABETH. Stop it.

KITTY. Well, she was so ordinary. So fucking ordinary.

ELIZABETH. It's me that's supposed to be disappointed.

KITTY. And aren't you? She wasn't exactly keen to re-acquaint herself with you was she?

ELIZABETH. I just wanted to know what happened.

KITTY. Wee spotty Kenny down at the swing park, that's what happened.

ELIZABETH. You don't know he had spots.

KITTY. Imagine never telling anyone, fourteen years old and giving birth in your bedroom while Coronation Street's on in the living-room.

ELIZABETH. She never said anything about Coronation Street.

KITTY. I'm just trying to make it more interesting for you.

ELIZABETH. She was just a child. She just wanted it all to go away.

KITTY. It? You.

ELIZABETH. Me.

KITTY. Still, she thought it was a very moving piece in the newspaper, 'very well written'. (*Pause.*) I suppose when you're adopted, the idea is that you get perfect parents to make up for being thrown away like a piece of litter.

ELIZABETH. I just wanted something that would make sense of everything.

KITTY. We had a really crap childhood, didn't we?

ELIZABETH. A lot of bad things happened. We were brought up on a battlefield.

KITTY. I'm glad you were there. Even if I didn't like you. You're still my sister. You'll always be my sister. I am sorry about Alec and everything. (*Awkwardly.*) I do love you.

ELIZABETH. You're not getting religion are you?

ELIZABETH *puts her head on* KITTY*'s shoulder.*

ELIZABETH. I suppose real love is where you have no choice.

KITTY. You make it sound like a prison sentence.

ELIZABETH. Have you ever been in love?

KITTY. Me? Don't be silly.

ELIZABETH. No, come on.

KITTY. Alec.

ELIZABETH. Poor Kitty.

Silence.

KITTY. I think it's going to rain.

Darkness.

Scene 10

The next day SUSIE *and* ELIZABETH *drinking.*

SUSIE. I just can't believe she did it. One minute we're talking about having a baby, talking about the future and the next she's gone off and got drunk, screwed some guy and got bloody pregnant. I mean, I could have done that, I could have screwed Callum. I had the offer. Unbelievable.

ELIZABETH. I didn't realise Jo liked blokes.

SUSIE. She doesn't. That's the bloody very unfunny joke. She did it to get pregnant. Her, the one who wanted everything all planned, no 'natural selection' for Dr Jo, oh no and then the next minute she's flat on her back with a fucking porter.

ELIZABETH. Where?

SUSIE. At a hospital do. Well, afterwards, in the car park or something equally sordid.

ELIZABETH. In the swing park.

SUSIE. What?

ELIZABETH. That's where I was conceived.

SUSIE. How do you know?

ELIZABETH. It doesn't matter, we're talking about you.

SUSIE. Don't be ridiculous. Have you met her? Have you seen her? Did she get in touch?

ELIZABETH. Yes.

SUSIE. And?

ELIZABETH (*shrugs*). And nothing really. She was, to use Kitty's words, 'so fucking ordinary'.

SUSIE. And that's it?

ELIZABETH. Yeah.

SUSIE. The biggest thing in your life. The thing you've been obsessing about forever.

ELIZABETH. Yeah.

SUSIE. Well at least you know who she is now. That was what you wanted. You got what you wanted, didn't you.

ELIZABETH. Let's not start fighting again. Please. I'm sorry, really.

SUSIE. We've never had a falling out before.

ELIZABETH. Well nothing in this life is constant, is it? I'm sorry.

The doorbell rings. ELIZABETH *answers,* CALLUM *enters.*

SUSIE. Oh look, it's Callum back from Ultima Thule.

CALLUM. I was in Shetland.

SUSIE. Yes, I know.

ELIZABETH. It's nine o'clock at night.

CALLUM. I know.

ELIZABETH. No, but I mean you haven't come to work?

CALLUM. Work? At this time of night?

SUSIE. Oh, let him in, he's one of the broken-hearted. Get
drunk with us, Callum. We are the unwanted of the world.
The abandoned. The chucked.

ELIZABETH. Susie's girlfriend left her and then got pregnant.

CALLUM. Nae luck.

SUSIE. And Elizabeth found her real mother –

CALLUM. Cool.

ELIZABETH. But she proved, oh what shall we say?
Unsatisfactory.

CALLUM. Sorry.

ELIZABETH. And oh yes, my boyfriend dumped me.

CALLUM. I never trusted him.

SUSIE. Bastard.

CALLUM. Laura's moving to Inverness. Taking Finn.

SUSIE. Bitch.

ELIZABETH. Inverness. What a strange idea. Perhaps that's
what we should do? Go north. Live in the country.

CALLUM. Keep chickens, goats. Grow all our own stuff.

SUSIE. No.

ELIZABETH. I thought I loved him. I did love him . . . I mean
it was a genuine emotion, it was an overwhelming emotion.
It was real. And yet it wasn't real. It's bizarre, isn't it? (*To*
SUSIE.) And you, the same. Exactly the same.

SUSIE. Thank you.

CALLUM. I love Laura.

SUSIE. I love Jo.

ELIZABETH. I love Alec.

SUSIE. What a load of shite.

ELIZABETH. In a year's time we probably won't still love them.

SUSIE. Oh, that makes me feel so much better.

ELIZABETH. In five years time we won't remember what they look like.

CALLUM. Does love ever last?

ELIZABETH. Well, I still love my dog.

SUSIE. God help us. Is that all we can look forward to? Everlasting love with the family pet.

CALLUM. I still love Finn.

ELIZABETH. People always love our kids.

SUSIE. Ina loves you.

CALLUM. And your parents don't dump you. (*To* ELIZABETH.) Except in your case, of course. Sorry.

Silence.

SUSIE (*to* ELIZABETH). If you could have one wish, right now, would it be to have Alec back?

ELIZABETH. One wish?

SUSIE. A selfish one. Not everybody to be happy and world peace and all that stuff.

CALLUM. And you can't wish for more wishes.

ELIZABETH. So many rules attached to this wish. (*Pause.*) I would wish . . . I would wish that God existed. That he was omnipotent and benevolent and that he did indeed mark the fall of every tiny sparrow.

CALLUM. Whoa. That's a fucking amazing wish.

Darkness.

Scene 11

AGNES (*following* MERRIC *around the room*). But why? You could leave her. We could run away. To Italy – or France.

MERRIC. Would you have me abandon everything?

AGNES. I would abandon everything for you.

MERRIC. You have nothing to abandon. My life is here. My profession, my wife, my children. My house. How could I just leave it all? I cannot give you what you want.

AGNES. What do I want?

MERRIC. You want eternal, undying love. And I cannot wander the continent like a Gypsy, like a beggar. Why on earth would I want to do that?

AGNES. For love.

MERRIC. You are my governess, for God's sake.

AGNES. It seems that I am your whore.

MERRIC. What you are is a woman who does not know her place.

AGNES. You have seduced me, sir.

MERRIC. You were more willing than any whore.

AGNES. Why are you so cruel? What we did was born of love. Of a true passion.

MERRIC. Don't fool yourself, fornication is fornication.

AGNES. I am carrying your child.

MERRIC. Then get rid of it.

AGNES. Get rid of it?

MERRIC. There are ways.

AGNES. I was not asking how. I have had the ways explained to me already.

MERRIC. Get rid of it, for God's sake.

AGNES. Do you not care for me at all? Do you have no feelings?

MERRIC. In truth? No. I care for you not one jot, Miss Soutar.

AGNES. You do not believe that, you do not mean those words. Why are you doing this? Are you such a coward that you cannot acknowledge your feelings for me? What will become of me?

MERRIC. You will be a fallen woman, Miss Soutar. You will pay the price of your conduct.

AGNES. And you will not?

MERRIC. You are to leave this house. Can you not see that?

AGNES. I shall tell your wife.

MERRIC. You think she does not know? You will go quietly, you will take your disgrace with you and leave. Do you understand?

AGNES. Do you think I will just go, as meek as a church mouse, as docile as a dog. I will shame you. I will haunt you.

LAETITIA *stands unnoticed in the doorway.*

AGNES. I will ruin you. I will drag you down with me. If there is to be no love then there will be retribution. I am going to cry your name on every street corner, down at your law courts, at your gentleman's club, at the Kirk, in the drawing-rooms of every acquaintance and friend you have. I shall turn up on the doorstep of Laetitia's genteel friends and tell them I am carrying your bastard child.

MERRIC. You cannot be anything but argumentative, Miss Soutar, I will stop your mouth. I will stop your words, your endless words.

AGNES. No you will not.

Enter LAETITIA.

LAETITIA. But I will.

LAETITIA *stabs* AGNES. *She falls and is caught by* MERRIC *who kisses her.*

Scene 12

The next morning. CALLUM *wakes up.*

CALLUM. Fuck.

　Enter SUSIE.

SUSIE. Dear God, how much did we drink?

CALLUM. A lot.

SUSIE. I feel like I've eaten an ashtray. I wasn't smoking as well, was I?

CALLUM. Half an ounce of dope.

SUSIE. God. I'm lucky to be alive.

CALLUM. Shall I make some coffee?

SUSIE (*opens the curtains*). What a lovely morning. The calm after the storm.

CALLUM. Sometimes I think that our real lives take place when we're asleep. And this is dreaming.

SUSIE. Oh, Callum, don't I've got a terrible headache.

CALLUM. This life, this real life, or this apparently real life, is just such a mess.

SUSIE. Callum.

CALLUM. What?

SUSIE. Shut up and make some coffee.

　ELIZABETH *enters.*

SUSIE. Hello, sleepyhead.

ELIZABETH. Oh God.

　CALLUM *trips on a floorboard.*

ELIZABETH. Someone's going to kill themselves on that.

CALLUM. Fucking hell. Come here.

ELIZABETH. What is it? Have you found something?

SUSIE. Buried treasure?

CALLUM. Not exactly. Look at this.

ELIZABETH. Oh, my God. (*Crosses herself.*)

SUSIE. We'd better phone the police.

Darkness.

Scene 13

Eight months later. CALLUM *taking photographs, everyone else sitting on the sofa in darkness. Flash.* SUSIE *holding the baby.*

INA. One with the grandmother holding the baby, I think. Let me get my hands on that little thing. (*Takes the baby.*) Who's a lovely little girl then? Who's a little pet?

KITTY (*to the baby*). No, diddums, it's all right, you are not a blood relative, you're not getting any of those granny genes.

INA. What is your Auntie Kitty talking about?

SUSIE. Shall I cut the cake?

INA. I don't know, a christening cake without a christening doesn't seem right.

ELIZABETH. It is if you don't believe in God.

INA. What a dreadful thing to say.

KITTY. No it's not. There's champagne in the fridge.

INA. I think I'd like a small sherry, please, if you've got one. Daddy always said don't drink anything that isn't brown.

KITTY. Did he, did he really?

INA (*to* ELIZABETH). I don't know how you're going to manage on your own.

ELIZABETH. I won't be on my own, I'll have the baby.

INA. Not a mother yet then, Susie? Maybe you could adopt? Can lesbians adopt? (*Whispers.*) Why is Callum here? He's got nothing to do with . . . the baby?

SUSIE. He's one of the family.

KITTY. He's renovating my flat.

SUSIE. That's what they're calling it nowadays, is it?

KITTY. Piss off.

INA. Not in front of the baby, please. I don't know how you could bring yourself to stay here, Elizabeth.

SUSIE. Why?

INA. Because of the (*Whispers.*) body.

SUSIE. The skeleton.

KITTY. Skeleton. That's a creepy word, isn't it?

CALLUM. It was quite a creepy thing.

INA. Oh, don't.

ELIZABETH. It's what we all become.

KITTY. It's what we all are. Bones. And flesh.

ELIZABETH. She was a real person.

INA. And you've never found out who she was? Or what happened to her?

SUSIE. She was murdered, that's what happened to her. You don't die a natural death under the floorboards.

INA. I thought history was your job.

SUSIE. I think she must have been a servant in the Chalmers' family. It's easier for the lower orders to disappear.

KITTY. Well, it wasn't one of the Chalmers' family, they're all accounted for in the family plot.

SUSIE. The investigative journalist.

KITTY. They were an interesting family actually.

INA. Who are we talking about?

SUSIE. Miss Aurora Chalmers.

INA. Who?

CALLUM. The old lady she bought the house off.

INA. Old lady?

ELIZABETH. Aurora's mother was Maude Chalmers. The artist?

INA. Never heard of her.

ELIZABETH. She had a sister called Edith.

KITTY. One of those lady explorers who hacked their way through jungles.

ELIZABETH. Cataloguing the flora and fauna of the world, fighting off crocodiles and capturing butterflies.

CALLUM. Butterflies?

INA (*to the baby*). I know, I know, you're being ignored. Poor little thing.

ELIZABETH. Why poor?

INA. Well she is a bastard. She doesn't look like you, does she look like her father?

KITTY. Alec.

ELIZABETH. I can't really remember what he looked like. I don't even have a photograph.

INA (*to* ELIZABETH). So, you've finally decided what to call her have you?

ELIZABETH. Agnes.

INA. Oh, what an old-fashioned name. Whatever made you think of that?

ELIZABETH. I don't know.

INA. You are strange.

CALLUM. Come on, smile, everybody, one last one for posterity. Say cheese.

KITTY (*getting up*). Do you need a cushion or something?

ELIZABETH. No thanks, I've got everything I need.

Flash, capturing them in disarray, followed by darkness. AGNES appears in the doorway carrying a candle. She blows the candle out.

Darkness.

"Seditious talk..."

Thinking of M's ideas that of his inferiority. Deep down he still is living off handouts & always will be. He has now married. Well B fears running away with love as he will end up like his parents. A wishes he would realise that it's not the end of the world to loose the life you know as it is ever changing. She wishes he could run off & sail into the sun set with her. Her mind is racing she loves him & longs to get caught up in the romanticism but knows deep down that he will never take the risk. She then start casting he religious beliefs

wide - questioning them so
that she can run to him.
She is longing to fold.
He is justifying the actions
he knows deep down that
she is going to take, that
he is going to regret.